PSYCHOLOGICAL ISSUES

VOL. VII, No. 4   MONOGRAPH 28

IMMEDIATE EFFECTS ON PATIENTS OF PSYCHOANALYTIC INTERPRETATIONS

by

EDITH LEVITOV GARDUK
and ERNEST A. HAGGARD

INTERNATIONAL UNIVERSITIES PRESS, INC.
239 Park Avenue South • New York, N. Y. 10003

PSYCHOLOGICAL ISSUES

HERBERT J. SCHLESINGER, *Editor*

Subscription per Volume, $15.00
Single Copies of This Number, $4.50

CONTENTS

ACKNOWLEDGMENTS

Much of this monograph, written in 1966, is based on a dissertation by the senior author submitted in partial fulfillment of the requirements for the Ph.D. degree at the University of Chicago. It was supported in part by grant MH-00637 from the National Institute of Mental Health, National Institutes of Health, United States Public Health Service.

The senior author wishes to acknowledge the valuable interest of and suggestions received from her dissertation advisory committee: William E. Henry, Allan Rechtschaffen, and Ernest A. Haggard. Special thanks are also extended to Kenneth S. Isaacs, Rosalind D. Cartwright, Sol Altschul, Brahm Baittle, Margery Baittle, Robert Lissitz, and Donald Baer for their helpfulness in certain phases of this research and to David Shakow for providing some data from the National Institute of Mental Health. In addition, appreciation is expressed to the therapists and patients who participated in this study but who must remain anonymous.

This monograph was prepared under the editorship of George S. Klein.

1

INTRODUCTION, DESIGN, AND HYPOTHESIS OF THE STUDY

In the realm of psychoanalysis much attention has been given to interpretation as a psychotherapeutic technique. Such topics as the appropriateness of presenting partial or relatively complete formulations, interpreting foreground or deeper-level material, emphasizing genetic or here-and-now connections, and pointing out or bypassing transference phenomena are extensively discussed. Opinions differ on many facets of interpretation, including its proper content, timing, sequence, dosage, depth, and form. In the broader domain of psychotherapy, even more controversial attention has been focused on interpretation. It is well-known, for instance, that "client-centered" clinicians view interpretation with disfavor. Thus, within and beyond the psychoanalytic fold, many theoretical positions have been taken with regard to interpretation and to its value. Interpretation is deemed either to be the sole curative tool of therapy, or to be the technique that is most disruptive of therapeutic progress, or to occupy various intermediate hero-villain roles between these extremes.

Despite this theoretical prominence, systematic investigations of the nature, role, effects, etc., of interpretations in psychotherapy have been sparse. Furthermore, for the psychoanalytically oriented clinician, much research that has been done is of limited value in that it is not optimally representative of the therapy process. In some research, the therapeutic interaction has been altered by laboratory procedures. Studies based on experimental paradigms of psychotherapy, controlled or standardized interviews, and artificially constructed therapist interventions modify—usually simplify—the conditions that are customarily encountered in daily clinical practice. In other instances, the work of inexperienced therapists has been examined, and study of their work does not provide the data of choice for judging psychotherapy techniques. The same limitation applies to research in which the therapists may have been experienced, but were not able or comfortable practitioners of the particular technique under survey: for example, basically client-centered counselors who make psychoanalytic interpretations. Apart from these several groups of studies only a very few empirical investigations of psychoanalytic interpretations have been reported.

In view of the meager data on reactions of patients to interpretations by professionally qualified and experienced psychoanalysts, further research in this area seemed worthwhile. Accordingly, the present study was undertaken with the purpose of investigating one facet of such reactions—the immediate effects on patients of psychoanalytic interpretations given in the course of their therapies.

DESIGN

Not surprisingly, a number of theoretical and practical questions arose at the inception of this research, and influenced its design and hypotheses. Of initial import was the selection of the experimental sample. Four of the cases that had been extensively recorded or filmed by the Psychotherapy Project of the University of Illinois College of Medicine seemed suitable for this investigation. Two of them were broadly classifiable as psychoanalyses and two as psychoanalytically oriented psychotherapies. They are described briefly in Appendix A. The therapists were all practicing analysts with formal training in psychoanalysis and many years of experience; the patients were psychoneurotic, above average in intelligence, and of middle-class socioeconomic status. Under these conditions, it was likely that these four therapies would include many genuine, typical interpretations. Whether the small number of cases would limit the generalizability of the study was a question of some concern. However, the investigators decided that the authenticity of the therapies, and hence their highly valid representation of "what happens in psychoanalytically oriented treatment," permitted generalization of a scientific nature. The acceptability and extent of such generalization is, of course, essentially a matter of individual research orientation and values. It may be mentioned here that the authenticity of even this highly valid material may have been impaired by the well-nigh inevitable reaction to recording or filming procedures (for a discussion of this topic, see Haggard et al., 1965).

Another initial and vital question was that of the best approach for investigating the effects of interpretations. How could such effects, determined as they are by a vast and fluctuating complex of interacting substantive and technical factors, be studied with any precision? The list of influences is formidable, even if only the relevant technical ones are considered. For instance, the effect of an interpretation may be determined by the state of the transference, the therapist's "tact" in presenting the interpretation, the structural level to which it is directed, its correctness, etc. The point of view could be taken, however, that the effect of a correct transference interpretation, or of a poorly timed interpretation of id impulses given during a positive transference phase, or of some other "subtype" of interpretation, did not merit primacy in empirical investigation. Because of the emphasis on interpretation as a certain type of intervention, it seemed logical first to ask, "Do patients react differently to interpretations than to other interventions, i.e., noninterpretations?" without pursuing more detailed distinctions. While the answer, of course, would be influenced by the kinds of interpretations studied, if any differences between the effects of interpretations and noninterpretations were marked and consistent, they should be apparent with this global approach. With this rationale, we adopted such an approach in the present research.

In addition to theoretical considerations, there were several practical reasons for posing the problem broadly. First, consensus concerning correctness, tact, etc., is difficult to obtain. Second, if the data must be divided finely, an adequate number of cases for each subtype requires a very large initial pool of data. A third reason derives from the experimental sample: given a group of skilled, experienced therapists, it may be assumed that their interpretations will tend to be specific, well timed, and generally appropriate. Under such conditions, many of the sources of variation mentioned above disappear. However, if this assumption is too optimistic, the emphasis need not be on interpretations that are correct or not, tactful or not, etc., but on interpretations that actually occur in competent psychotherapy. The effects of such characteristic interpretations merit study as a group without further subdivision.

Having decided to compare interpretations with noninterpretations, it seemed advantageous to draw them, in pairs, from the same therapy hours. This procedure was a conservative one—a comparison of reactions to interventions from the same hour was hardly likely to yield great differences, and especially so since only brief response periods (see below) were studied. However, if differences were found despite this essentially unpropitious arrangement, they would indeed be worthy of attention. Furthermore, such a design allowed for the control of "irrelevant variation"— factors that were essentially extraneous to the comparison of the two intervention types. For example, if the patient was in a negative transference phase, he would probably continue so throughout a given hour; accordingly, the influence of the state of the transference on the paired interpretation and noninterpretation would be the same. Similarly, if in a given hour the therapist tended to be awkward in his formulations, or especially well timed in his comments, such therapist variables would be broadly equivalent for the paired interpretation and noninterpretation. Patient factors such as the influence of a current life stress (e.g., beginning a new job), a passing daily mood (e.g., elation), a certain subject of discussion (e.g., family quarrels), a focal conflict (e.g., autonomy struggles), and so forth, would also be roughly equated for the two types of intervention. In brief, many of the sources of variation that were a function of the larger therapy and extratherapy context were eliminated through this procedure.

Cause and effect delineations also were considered in designing the study. While one may observe and measure various responses of patients in psychotherapy, it is difficult to determine exactly what caused them, because of the complexity of the situation. Strictly speaking, the evidence that was available in the present study was that interpretations were followed by such and such patient behavior, not that such and such patient behavior was caused by interpretations. Nevertheless, our methodology attempted to equalize or randomize possible determinants of patient reactions other than the interpretation or noninterpretation that preceded them. Since the only aspect of the situation that was systematically varied was the selected intervention, the inference was made that patient reactions were a function of it and caused by it.

It is obvious that interventions by therapists may have long-range as well as immediate effects. While both of these are of interest, this study was directed only at the latter, with "immediate" defined as encompassing the five minutes of the therapy hour following the selected intervention. Thus, the five minutes following each interpretation or noninterpretation constituted the "effect period" that was studied to determine the influence of the preceding intervention on the patient. Although five minutes may seem to be arbitrary, there was good justification for its use, once the decision was made to sample only a relatively brief time period. This period had to be long enough for effects to be detectable, but not so long that the effects might be dissipated. Preliminary work showed that less than five minutes might yield insufficient patient material if there was much silence or if the therapist was very active. Accordingly, a five-minute period was indicated as the most useful one for this study.

The procedure of comparing patient reactions during the five minutes following an interpretation with those during the five minutes following a noninterpretation may be naïve from the standpoint of psychic equivalence. That is, although the time units are physically comparable, it does not follow that they are psychically comparable. It might well be that one should compare the 20 minutes, or the 24 hours, following an interpretation with the five minutes following a noninterpretation. The point is made here, however, that lacking more information one may well start with equivalent temporal units, and with "immediate" defined as within five minutes.

A number of effect variables were selected for study. Several of these pertained to form qualities of verbal activity by patients. These were chosen because of interest in questions such as, "Do interpretations stimulate patients to talk?" "Do they silence them?" In addition, the ease of accurately measuring various form qualities, and the usefulness of such measures as base lines for comparison with other form and content variables, were also considered.

The second and larger group of effects that were of interest could be classified as content variables. Some were selected from descriptions in the literature of immediate, typical, frequent, or noticeable reactions of patients to interpretations. Others were included as concepts that analytically oriented therapists almost invariably refer to in discussing their patients. Many of the content variables were difficult to define precisely. Partly because of this, a few of them were not completely independent of the others. Nevertheless, each content variable studied was considered to communicate some unique information, especially if viewed within the traditional psychoanalytic framework.

Further methodological considerations and decisions will be presented in their appropriate context later. Here let us briefly describe the final form of the research design: interpretations and noninterpretations were drawn from psychoanalytically oriented psychotherapies. For a given hour one interpretation plus the following five minutes of the psychotherapy session was paired with one noninterpretation plus the following five minutes of the psychotherapy session. The interpretation selected was the most comprehensive interpretation in the hour. The noninterpretation was whatever intervention (excluding interpretations) occurred closest to 10 minutes earlier in the same hour. To determine how patients reacted in the five minutes following these interventions, two broad areas of effect were studied. These consisted of various form and content qualities that are frequently mentioned by analysts and other therapists.

HYPOTHESES

The specific hypotheses of the study are stated here. They are phrased positively rather than in the traditional null form, but were tested by the usual statistical methods.

For all form variables, differences are postulated between the effects of interpretations and noninterpretations. No directions are predicted for these differences because of the lack of theoretical and empirical evidence favoring one result over another. In contrast, hypotheses for the content variables are phrased positively and in one direction. With one exception (Hypothesis 12), more of the given effect is predicted after interpretations than after noninterpretations. This procedure leads to some apparent contradictions. For example, how can there be both more depression and more pleasant affect after interpretations than after noninterpretations? The answer lies both in the nature of psychoanalytic theory and in the methodology of the present research. Thus, interpretations may at one time elicit one emotion, at another time another. Furthermore, phenomena such as ambivalence and different affects at different inferential levels are not rare in psychoanalytic formulations. With regard to the research design, since the effect period encompassed five minutes of the psychotherapy hour, there was enough time for a variety of reactions to take place. The most cogent point here, however, is that the relevant comparison was between paired interpretation data and noninterpretation data; thus, one might postulate either more dysphoric or more euphoric affect, or both, following interpretations than following the paired noninterpretations.

The brief theoretical discussions that accompany each hypothesis include references to empirical work of some relevancy. With few exceptions, these are quite different from the present study in definitions, methodology, orientation, etc.[1] Where comparisons of findings seem directly appropriate they are made in later discussion sections. Note that in all of the hypotheses except the first one, the phrases "following interpretations" and "following noninterpretations" refer to the period within five minutes of the specified intervention.

Hypothesis 1. The reaction times of patients to interpretations are different from their reaction times to noninterpretations. Since the early 1900s many studies of reaction time have demonstrated its usefulness as a sign of emotional involvement. A response time to individual words that is longer than average is a common signal of personal disturbance, but sometimes a very short response time is a complex indicator (Bell, 1948). In the present study, interpretations are hypothesized to be more emotionally arousing than

---

[1] The investigations that are most similar to the present one in some of the kinds of cases and some of the variables studied are those of Auld and White (1959), Lennard and Bernstein (1960), and Speisman (1957).

noninterpretations. However, whether personal involvement is manifested by especially quick or especially slow reaction times probably depends on the defensive make-up of the individual patient. Accordingly, no directional prediction is made about whether patients will take more or less time to react to interpretations. For empirical data of some relevance to this hypothesis, see a verbal conditioning study by Adams, Butler, and Noblin (1962).

Hypothesis 2. The verbal activity of patients after interpretations differs in amount from their verbal activity after noninterpretations. In psychoanalytic theory, it is customarily asserted that interpretations bring forth new responses from patients. Since such new responses may take many different forms, including additional associations or silence, it is difficult to predict whether interpretations elicit increased or decreased verbalization by the patient. Nevertheless, it is postulated that there is some marked change in the amount of verbalization after interpretations as compared with that after noninterpretations. Among the empirical studies of relevance to this hypothesis are those of Butler (1962); Colby (1961); Kanfer, Phillips, Matarazzo, and Saslow (1960); and Lennard and Bernstein (1960).

Hypothesis 3. The amount of silence of patients after interpretations differs from the amount of their silence after noninterpretations. If interventions by the therapist influence verbalizations by the patient, they must of necessity also influence his pauses or silence. Since silence on the part of the patient is a concept of some theoretical importance, however, it is treated as a separate topic. When the patient is silent, he is violating the fundamental psychoanalytic rule of saying whatever comes to mind. Silence, therefore, traditionally has been viewed as one manifestation of resistance. Silence is also frequently considered to be an index of anxiety. But whether it is viewed as a form of resistance, as an anxiety indicator, or as serving other functions during a psychotherapy hour, it is likely to vary in relation to what the therapist says. Empirical work with silence and interpretations has been done by Auld and White (1959), Lennard and Bernstein (1960), and Mahl (1961).

Hypothesis 4. Patients manifest more affect after interpretations than after noninterpretations. Affect is a variable of fundamental importance in psychotherapy. It is considered generally here, in terms of the presence or discharge of any kind of affect. Subsequent hypotheses deal with specific affects. No matter what theoretical orientation is espoused it is generally agreed that "interpretations have affective consequences" (Levy, 1963, p. 253). It is when particular affects are postulated that theoretical biases emerge. For some data on "affective propositions" by patients and interpretive material by therapists, see Lennard and Bernstein (1960, p. 140).

Hypothesis 5. Patients manifest more anxiety after interpretations than after noninterpretations. Many theorists cite anxiety as a typical response to an interpretation (Horney in Slater, 1956; Paul, 1963; Sullivan, 1947). Although the predominant view specifies increased anxiety immediately after an interpretation, the matter is complex (Isaacs, 1939; Strachey, 1934) and opinion is far from unanimous on this point. For example, Saul (1958) states, "A properly made interpretation relieves rather than increases the patient's anxiety" (p. 154). The empirical work of Dibner (1958) and Pope and Siegman (1962) is somewhat germane to Hypothesis 5.

Hypothesis 6. Patients manifest more anger, hostility, or aggression after interpretations than after noninterpretations. Interpretations may arouse anger and resentment in the patient in a number of circumstances. For instance, such feelings may occur if interpretations are superficial (Greenson, 1959), if they are correct (Fromm-Reichmann, 1951), or if they are disturbing (Alexander and French, 1946).

Hypothesis 7. Patients manifest more depression, morbid or dysphoric affect after interpretations than after noninterpretations. Since interpretation often "leads to the reactivation of painful tendencies, memories, and conflicts" (Bibring, 1954, p. 758), the patient may well feel depressed or sorrowful in reaction to it. Indeed, in many instances feelings of sadness are highly appropriate. The patient can now permit himself to experience—rather than repress or displace—an unhappy, still potent memory. But, besides the reactivation of painful memories, there is a broader basis for dysphoric affect. An interpretation may deprive the patient in some way. Tarachow (1963), for example, states that "the principal consequence (of an interpretation) is object loss. A correct interpretation is followed by a mild depression" (p. 20).

Hypothesis 8. Patients manifest more pleasant affect after interpretations than after noninterpretations. Interpretations may elicit relief, gratification, feelings of reassurance, or other pleasant affect from the patient. There are two major explanations for the occurrence of pleasant affect. One emphasizes the relief of inner tension through affect discharge and increased understanding. The other stresses direct gratification from the therapist's empathy, "gift," etc. However, with regard to this latter explanation, certain types of noninterpretations—such as reassurances or expressions of interest—probably are more directly gratifying to patients than are interpretations. Thus, this explanation would favor the proposition that noninterpretations would be followed by more pleasant affect than interpretations. Nevertheless, in keeping with the psychoanalytic framework of this research, preference is given to the first explanation and to the hypothesis as stated. Work by Snyder (1963) is of some relevance to Hypothesis 8.

Hypothesis 9. Patients manifest more surprise after interpretations than after noninterpretations. Theoretical discussions of the effects of interpretations almost invariably state that interpretations often produce a feeling of surprise (Brenner, 1955; Colby, 1951; Greenson, 1959). Hypothesis 9 reflects this emphasis, although surprise is not exclusive to interpretations. Thus, Bibring (1954) points out, "As a rule patients react to (successful) clarification with surprise and intellectual satisfaction" (p. 757).

Hypothesis 10. Patients manifest more ego dysfunctioning after interpretations than after noninterpretations. Several ways in which interpretations may be disturbing have already been noted. A more global concept of disturbance or disruption is subsumed under such terms as ego dysfunctioning or ego disorganization. These terms are used by clinicians; patients may describe themselves as "falling apart" or "disintegrating" (Palombo and Bruch, 1964). It is almost inevitable that certain moments and phases of psychotherapy will be traumatic to the patient. This is particularly true in psychoanalytic treatment where there is much "uncovering" and old defenses can no longer be used, but new alignments of id, ego, and superego are fragile. Such traumatic moments may well occur in reaction to interpretations.

Hypothesis 11. Patients manifest more alterations in symptoms or aggravation of symptoms after interpretations than after noninterpretations. According to psychoanalytic theory, many symptoms are substitute phenomena. That is, they occur as a consequence of the repression of certain experiences and affects. It seems highly likely, therefore, that interpretations by the therapist that are directed at latent material will influence manifest symptoms. Many writers have pointed out that interpretations may be followed by alterations in both the form and the intensity of symptoms (Christiansen, 1964; Kubie, 1960; Loewenstein, 1963). Freud (1937) stated that under conditions of a negative therapeutic reaction the patient will react to a correct construction[2] "with an unmistakable aggravation of his symptoms and of his general condition" (p. 265).

Hypothesis 12. Patients communicate less relatively factual, conscious-level material after interpretations than after noninterpretations. Interpretations, by definition, deal with material that is at least partly at the nonmanifest level. If the patient "processes" interpretations, it seems likely that his communication will deal with such material and at the same time his comments on factual, conscious material will decrease. For data that are somewhat pertinent to this hypothesis, i.e., studies of "statements about the problem," see Frank and Sweetland (1962).

Hypothesis 13. Patients communicate more relatively subjective, deeper-level material after interpretations than after noninterpretations. Freud (1937) indicated that one confirmation of a construction "is implied . . . when the patient answers with an association which contains something similar or analogous to the content of the construction" (p. 263). This type of association would probably fall in the category of deeper-level material studied here. However, regardless of whether the patient confirms the interpretation or not, one customarily postulated effect of interpretations is that they elicit new material from the patient in the form of memories, fantasies, dreams, and observations of inner feelings and reactions.

---

[2] Freud's "constructions" are classified as interpretations in the present study.

Data on "self-observation" that are particularly germane to this topic have been presented by Cartwright (1966).

Hypothesis 14. Patients manifest more blocking of associations or difficulty in producing associations after interpretations than after noninterpretations. Blocking of associations is one of the many forms of resistance in psychotherapy, and may well follow an interpretation, particularly if the material is difficult for the patient to accept. Blocking includes those reactions of the patient that indicate he is in some way unable to recognize or talk about the idea just presented. Some data on "emotional blocking" have been reported by Gillespie (1953).

Hypothesis 15. Patients have more oppositional and defensive associations after interpretations than after noninterpretations. This hypothesis is phrased in terms of oppositional and defensive associations, rather than in terms of the broader concept of manifestations of resistance. Nevertheless, it refers to what is really the essence of resistance: verbalization by the patient that seems to originate "from unconscious defenses against the material being made conscious" (Bibring, 1954, p. 756). Resistance has been studied by Auld and White (1959), Robert and Mabel Cohen (1961), Gillespie (1953), and Speisman (1957).

Hypothesis 16. Patients manifest more understanding and insight after interpretations than after noninterpretations. "The purpose of an interpretation is to produce knowledge or insight in the patient" (Shulman, Kaspar, and Barger, 1964, p. 114). So say psychoanalytically oriented therapists. A clearly divergent point of view is espoused by nondirective theorists. Rogers (1942) states that "insight is often delayed, and sometimes made impossible, by efforts of the counselor to create it or bring it about" (p. 195). With such distinctly opposite opinions, it is not surprising that understanding and insight, defined in various ways, have been investigated by a number of experimenters, including Bergman (1951), Dittman (1952), Frank and Sweetland (1962), Grossman (1952), Sherman (1945), and Snyder (1945).

Hypothesis 17. Patients deal with more transference-related material after interpretations than after noninterpretations. Although definitions of transference vary, the more traditional position is presented by Menninger (1958), who describes transference as "the unrealistic roles or identities unconsciously ascribed to a therapist by a patient in the regression of the psychoanalytic treatment and the patient's reactions to this representation derived from earlier experience" (p. 81). According to psychoanalytic theory, changes in the patient are most closely related to the analysis and working through of the transference. It follows from this that many of the interpretations of the therapist are "transference-related." Indeed, such interpretations are often considered the most powerful interventions in the therapeutic armamentarium. In the present study, because of the nature of the sample, it is assumed that many interpretations will be explicitly or implicitly directed at the transference. The further assumption—that if the patient is dealing with this therapist input, his references to transference material will increase—provides the rationale for Hypothesis 17.

2

GENERAL PROCEDURE

DEFINITION OF INTERPRETATIONS

Interpretation is here defined as a psychotherapeutic intervention that has two major emphases: (1) on explanation, and (2) dealing with unconscious material. Interpretations are explanatory in nature; they bring meaning or intelligibility to a patient's productions. This "supplying of a missing factor" (Murphy, 1958, p. 448) as a major aid to the patient's comprehension of his behavior constitutes a first necessary criterion for interpretation. No precise convention exists for separating interpretations from such other interventions as confrontations and "preparations for interpretation." However, the stipulation that interpretations have greater reference than other interventions to that which is unconscious or preconscious in the patient establishes the second distinguishing criterion for this category of therapist activity. The actual content of interpretations concerns such phenomena as resistance, defenses, affects, impulses, transference, conflicts, dynamics, personality traits, physical reactions, gestures, symbols, and dreams.

The validity of this definition is indicated by its general conformation with the view of interpretation cited by Bibring (1954), part of which follows:

> Interpretation . . . refers exclusively to unconscious material: to the unconscious defensive operations (motives and mechanisms of defense), to the unconscious, warded-off instinctual tendencies, to the hidden meanings of the patient's behavior patterns, to their unconscious interconnections, etc. . . . in contrast to clarification, interpretation by its very nature transgresses the clinical data, the phenomenological-descriptive level. On the basis of their derivatives, the analyst tries to "guess" and to communicate

16

(to explain) to the patient in form of (hypothetical) constructions and reconstructions those unconscious processes which are assumed to determine his manifest behavior [p. 757].

For a more operational definition of interpretation the two major aspects of the theoretical definition are, in a sense, quantified. This quantification is done by stipulating, first, that one or more specific connections be made between various patient elements—thoughts, feelings, behaviors, dreams, or other phenomena. Second, these connections must be more than simple similarities or juxtapositions; that is, they must include some reference to non-manifest material.

Furthermore, it is also convenient to group various patient phenomena into a larger framework consisting of four major categories:

Past Reference	Present Reference
surface material	surface material
deep material	deep material

An interpretation considered in relation to this model might connect elements in all four of these categories, or, again, it might connect several elements within any one of these categories. If only manifest elements are connected, it is the interconnection itself (rather than the elements) of which the patient is deemed to be unconscious.

Because interpretations inevitably differ in the relative totality of relationships, patterning, and ramifications they embrace, they can be classified on a comprehensive-moderate-limited continuum of scope. Even though the primary focus of the study is on interpretations and noninterpretations, it also considers this subclassification of interpretations. The following three levels of comprehensiveness are specified:

Comprehensive. The flavor of a comprehensive interpretation is that of relating many aspects of the phenomenon under scrutiny. Frequently a comprehensive interpretation ties together, in considerable detail, references to present surface material, past surface material, present deep material, and past deep material. Because of their inclusiveness and detail, such interpretations are often lengthy (but not every long interpretation is a comprehensive one).

Moderate. These interpretations vary more in scope than do comprehensive ones. At most, a moderate interpretation ties together past, present, surface, and deep elements by implication or in minimal detail. More frequently, it is not so encompassing. At the least, a moderate interpretation makes more than one connection within or between the four reference categories.

Limited. A limited interpretation is less than a moderate interpretation in its explanatory inclusiveness. It is clearly an interpretation, but it makes only one connection within or between past, present, surface, and deep material.

Since we were interested in the most inclusive interpretations available in the data, this study is confined as far as possible to comprehensive and moderate interpretations. Examples from psychotherapy hours of the three categories of interpretations are presented in Appendix B.

Certain limitations of the present study, due to the definition of interpretation that was used, may be pointed out:

1. The study does not include nonverbal interpretations, such as interpretive gestures, nor interpretations conveyed primarily by vocal inflections of the therapist, nor interpretations that are implied.

2. Interpretations have to be considered only within the context of an hour; they cannot be judged from other hours, or knowledge of the patient's history or psychological tests.

3. Since interpretations deal with phenomena of which the patient is in some way unconscious, the patient's material in the psychotherapy hour must be read and considered carefully. From such reading often one can only say that the patient does not verbalize, integrate, or imply something, and hence seems not to be aware of it. Accordingly, an inference has to be made about whether or not he is unconscious of certain material.

DEFINITION OF NONINTERPRETATIONS

Briefly, noninterpretations are those interventions by therapists that are not classifiable as interpretations. A more positive statement about noninterpretations can be made, however, by indicating the senior author's general frame of reference with regard to classifying interventions. Before undertaking this study, she had rated a number of psychotherapy hours, using several different coding systems, including those of Bales (1950), Cartwright (1966),[1] Rogers and Rablen (1958), and Sklansky et al. (1960, 1966). The use of Cartwright's scale, "Therapist's Response re Patient's Self-Observation," provided particularly useful experience.[2] The scale consisted of seven categories: six delineated interventions other than interpretations; the seventh category referred to "interpretations." It was implicitly on the basis of this previous work that the senior author classified an intervention as a noninterpretation in the present research. The explicit basis, not fitting the criteria for an interpretation, has already been mentioned.

SELECTION OF INTERPRETATIONS

Fifteen suitable interpretations from each case were considered to constitute an adequate sample. To obtain these the investigator read transcripts of randomly selected hours, keeping in mind the definition and criteria for interpretations. If no comprehensive or moderate interpretation was found in an hour, it was discarded from the study. In gathering the data only one interpretation was selected from any one hour. If more than one interpretation occurred in an hour, the most inclusive one was chosen, since the experimental sample consisted of "best" interpretations, and "best" was defined in this study in terms of inclusiveness. If several interpretations of equal quality occurred in an hour, the earliest one was selected for the study.

Reading continued until at least four clearly comprehensive interpretations and at least 11 moderate interpretations were selected for each case, except for Case 3. For Case 3, suitable interpretations were so infrequent that it was not possible to adhere to the specified standards. To obtain enough selections for this case, the investigator had to use interpretations that were less inclusive

---

[1] Cartwright has indicated that this system is an implementation of a paper by Arthur A. Miller et al. (1965).

[2] On this scale a reliability of approximately 88% had been established between Cartwright and the senior author.

than those for the other cases. Thus, the 15 interpretations from Case 3 consisted of no comprehensive interpretations, five moderate interpretations, and 10 interpretations that were initially classified as moderate but were on the border between moderate and limited. Later these were considered to be limited.

In all, 333 hours were read and 76 interpretations selected. The 16 extra interpretations (from Cases 1 and 2) were then eliminated, on the basis either of less inclusive scope or of insufficient postinterpretation time available. The final experimental sample of 60 interpretations is presented in Table 1.

Problem of the Unit

In reading the psychotherapy hours, it became clear that interpretations may consist of one numbered therapist statement[3] only (T 27, for instance), a consecutive or nearly consecutive sequence of two or more numbered statements (T 27, T 28, T 30), or two or more statements distinctly separated by intervening therapist or patient material (T 27, T 55). The first two of the above were treated as single interpretations, since each consists of an essentially unbroken unity; in contrast, the material in the last instance was treated as two separate interpretations. Accordingly, the unit for this study is the interpretation (interpretation sequence) rather than each numbered therapist statement. Throughout this book, "intervention" refers to however many numbered therapist statements constitute the selected interpretation or noninterpretation.

Once the interpretation could extend over a variable number of therapist statements, i.e., once there was an interpretive sequence, it became necessary to establish certain conventions about where such a sequence began and ended. The investigator tried to limit each interpretive sequence to the essential "heart" of the interpretation. This meant not including preparations for the interpretation or preliminary aspects of the interpretation, such as redirective comments or clarifications of content. Also not included were repetitions or minor nonsignificant enlargements of the interpreta-

---

[3] Therapist statements were numbered sequentially in the typescripts. A therapist statement or remark consisted of all therapist material that occurred between two patient remarks.

TABLE 1

IDENTIFICATION OF PSYCHOTHERAPY HOURS, INTERPRETATIONS, AND NONINTERPRETATIONS

Therapy Hour	Interpretations	Noninterpretations	Therapy Hour	Interpretations	Noninterpretations
	Case 1			Case 2	
9	183-186	108-111	73	30	17
13	159	116[b]	100	44	34
14	176-183[a]	107-114	121	12-16	5-8[c]
23	124-129	75-80	137	16	12[b]
24	106-108[a]	55-57	148	15	8
32	174	126	157	21-22	15-16
37	87-88	58-59	158	7	2
44	84	52	210	6[a]	3
45	118-120[a]	87-89[b]	222	8	1
58	122-123	94-95	234	5[a]	2
68	66	15	257	11-12[a]	2-3
78	170-174	143-147	282	7-8	2-3
80	124-129[a]	59-64	287	16-17	6-7
98	131	103	288	14-18	3-7
129	100-104	41-45[b]	305	27[a]	13
	Case 3			Case 4	
31	12-17	6[c]	3	49-50	40-41
38	23-24	12-13	6	62-65	45-48
40	29	20	8	67	42
42	19	14	9	42-44	37-39
60	25	19	10	40-43	20-23
68	22-28	9-12[b,c]	12	71-75	39-43[b]
70	23	16[b]	18	69-73[a]	34-38
75	35	25[b]	19	70-74[a]	26-30
625	37	18	20	58-64	35-41
627	41-43	25-27	23	27-29	8-10
630	33-34	20-21[b]	24	51-56[a]	6-11[b]
637	36	30	25	80-83	55-58[b]
640	42-44	33-34[c]	29	116-118	74-76
644	60	48	33	139-140	102-103[b]
645	33-34	22-23	34	26-29[a]	2-4[c]

[a]Comprehensive interpretation.   [b]Close noninterpretation.

[c]Not possible to excerpt same number of therapist statements for noninterpretation sequence as for interpretation sequence.

tion. Decisions about the beginning and ending of an interpretation were, in the final analysis, arbitrary. However, attempts were made to detail defining criteria closely enough so that consensus could be obtainable later.

SELECTION OF NONINTERPRETATIONS

After all interpretations had been selected, noninterpretations were selected from the same hours (Table 1). This was done by timing tape recordings of the hours to establish a 10-minute interval before the interpretation, and then taking the first therapist intervention immediately before that 10 minutes, excluding interpretations and contentless interventions.[4] If an interpretation for an hour consisted of more than one numbered therapist statement, the same number of therapist statements was selected to constitute the noninterpretation. For several hours the 10-minute interval was shortened because of technical or substantive conditions that could not be regulated.[5]

When all noninterpretations had been selected, it was apparent that they included a range of therapist remarks. Most of them were requests for information, didactic statements, and simple clarifications; a few were reflections and "clarifications plus"—clarifications with an additional evaluative or implicitly explanatory element contributed by the therapist. The former group seemed to be far from interpretations on the interpretive continuum, and the latter seemed to be close to interpretations. Since a

---

[4] A constant error could be introduced into the data by always selecting noninterpretations that occurred before interpretations. That is, as a psychotherapy hour continues, certain patient reactions might begin and increase as a function of time, rather than as a function of a particular intervention by the therapist. However, this hardly seemed a major obstacle if only 10 minutes elapsed between the two interventions studied (and the interval is even briefer if it is measured from the end of the effect period following the first intervention). An alternative procedure—having some of the noninterpretations follow the interpretations—was undesirable, both because the possibility of confounding effects was greater and because interpretations tended to occur toward the end of psychotherapy sessions.

[5] Eight hours were timed at a different location under the procedure of an eight-minute interval between interventions. In a few other instances only contentless interventions ("M'hm," "Ah-h") occurred more than 10 minutes earlier. In still other infrequent instances, the interpretation was given so early that 10 minutes had not elapsed since the beginning of the hour.

classification of all noninterpretations as either "far" or "close" seemed useful, they were so classified. Examples of these two categories of noninterpretations are presented in Appendix B.

ESTABLISHMENT OF FREEDOM FROM SELECTION BIAS, RELIABILITY, AND VALIDITY IN CONNECTION WITH INTERPRETATIONS AND NONINTERPRETATIONS

The problem of selection bias arose because in going through the psychotherapy hours, the investigator read both the interventions by the therapist and the responses by the patient. Therefore, it was possible that only interpretations to which patients reacted in a certain way had been selected, perhaps unknowingly. The argument that interpretations occurred so infrequently that one would be unlikely to omit any suggested impartiality but was hardly conclusive. It was now necessary to have an independent judge also pick the most comprehensive interpretations in various sessions. Since the judge would be unacquainted with the purposes of this study, presumably his selection of interpretations would not be based on a certain type of reaction. If his choices concurred with the investigator's, lack of selection bias would be indicated.

Reliability would be indicated if at least two people agreed highly in their classification of the study material into interpretations and noninterpretations. This could be accomplished by presenting certain interventions and asking, "Which kind of intervention is it?" However, the more difficult procedure of having a judge read entire hours for interpretations would not only provide evidence of reliability, but in addition would answer questions of selection bias and validity. With regard to the latter: since interpretation as used here is essentially a psychoanalytic concept, it was desirable that the interpretations of the study be acceptable as such to psychoanalysts. It seemed preferable, therefore, that the judge be a psychoanalyst; if he agreed on the interpretations, the data would be considered valid.

To provide information on these matters, the investigator selected a sample of 24 hours from the four cases. It was judged that six of these hours contained no interpretations, six contained comprehensive interpretations, and the remaining 12 contained a range of moderate interpretations. These unidentified hours, definitions, and instructions were given to a psychoanalyst who was asked to list all interpretations of moderate or comprehensive scope, to designate and classify the most comprehensive interpretation in each hour, and to make any comments he considered relevant.

The first 16 hours that the psychoanalyst-judge classified and returned included the six that had been designated as containing no interpretations and these were put aside. In the other 10 hours, while the judge had selected interpretations which in each instance encompassed the same material as the investigator's, he frequently (in eight out of the 10 hours) had taken a larger portion of the hour. For instance, where the investigator had chosen "T 8-T 11 inclusive" as the most comprehensive interpretation in the hour, the judge chose "T 7-T 13 inclusive" as the most comprehensive interpretation in the hour.

Before seeing the remaining eight hours (but after having been told by the judge that they all contained interpretations), the investigator gave the judge further instructions with the aim of obtaining more comparable units. The judge was again requested to pick only the essential content, the "heart" of the most comprehensive interpretation. Furthermore, he was asked to confine that selection to the exact number of consecutive therapist statements now designated for each hour.[6]

The results of the judging procedure may be summarized as follows. For the 18 hours considered to contain interpretations, the judge picked *precisely* the same interpretations as the investigator 16 times. In one instance of disagreement, the judge had initially missed the interpretation in question; when asked about it later he labeled it a limited one. In the other instance, he picked as the most inclusive interpretation in the hour a repetition and enlargement of the interpretation chosen by the investigator. For the six hours considered to contain no interpretations, the judge considered four of them to contain no interpretations, one to contain a limited interpretation, and one to contain a moderate interpretation. The latter was qualified with the following comment: "Interpretation borders on limited side." Both of these had been considered as "clarifications plus" by the investigator.

---

[6] For example, for hour 29 he was to select a sequence of eight therapist statements; for hour 57, five statements; for hour 600, three statements, etc.

Over-all, there were agreements in 20 of the 24 hours of the sample on the exact selection of interpretations or noninterpretations. This degree of agreement, 83%, is satisfactory for this type of material. However, if the basis for evaluation had been the number of therapist statements in an hour with the rationale that this was the number of judgments that actually had to be made, the agreement would be far greater than the figures indicate. In any event, lack of selection bias, reliability in selecting interpretations and noninterpretations, and validity were considered to be adequately established.

Reliability of Subclassification of Data

Although the instructions to the judge had indicated that this study was primarily concerned with comprehensive and moderate interpretations, he included limited interpretations in his evaluation of the hours. In addition, he made many comments such as "Borders on limited," "Almost limited," "May be a limited interpretation—I probably stretched it a little," "Possibly moderate but really believe this is just a limited interpretation." While these comments applied to all cases, they predominated for Case 3.

The independent designations of the material in the reliability study as comprehensive, moderate, limited, or noninterpretation yielded 17 agreements out of 24 hours, or 71% agreement. This agreement could be increased to 79% by combining the moderate and limited categories. Accordingly, these categories were combined. The subclassification of data now became comprehensive interpretations and moderate-limited interpretations.

Some disagreements had also occurred about the distinction between comprehensive and moderate interpretations. Since comprehensive interpretations were so rare, all of them were given for evaluation to another judge—an experienced, psychoanalytically trained psychotherapist with a Ph.D. in psychology. The final classification was then based on the designation given by two out of three raters (see Table 1).

Additional Reliability Study

After these judging procedures, each selected intervention was typed on a separate card without identification and without accompanying context. These cards were given to another qualified psychologist for classification. The results of this reliability check follow:

1. Classification into interpretations and noninterpretations—113 out of 120 interventions or 94% agreement; Pearson $r = .90$ ($p < .001$).

2. Subclassification into comprehensive interpretations, moderate-limited interpretations, and noninterpretations—105 out of 120 interventions or 88% agreement; Pearson $r = .85$ ($p < .001$).

DETERMINATION OF FIVE-MINUTE EFFECT PERIOD AND OTHER TIMINGS

The selection of interpretations and noninterpretations provided only part of the basic data for this study. To investigate the immediate effects of such interventions, it was necessary to excerpt from the psychotherapy hours the five minutes following each of them. This required timing tape recordings of the hours. Since timing of part of the material was also necessary in order to study certain form variables, the timing procedure will be described in the general sequence in which it was performed.

The typescript of a given hour was marked to indicate the beginning and ending of the selected noninterpretation, and the beginning and ending of the selected interpretation. Since the noninterpretation occurred earlier in the hour, it was located first on the corresponding tape recording. By listening to the tape, reading the typescript of the tape, and using a stop watch, one could mark on the transcript the duration of each numbered remark by the therapist and by the patient and the duration of pauses within and between remarks. A manually operated stop watch was used and no attempt was made to measure more precisely than one second—i.e., if a person spoke for less than one second, the notation on the typescript was for one second. All material from the beginning to the end of the noninterpretation was timed (this could include several numbered therapist and patient remarks). These timings were considered "intervention-period" timings. Timing of the five-minute period following the noninterpretation began at the end of the "intervention period." Again, the duration of each remark by the therapist and by the patient, and pauses within and between remarks, were noted. These timings continued until five minutes had elapsed, and were considered "effect-period" timings.

The same procedure was carried out for the interpretation in the same hour.[7]

In 10 of the hours[8] it was not possible to obtain a full five-minute effect period following the selected interpretation since these sessions ended before five minutes had elapsed. Whenever such a curtailed effect period occurred, the effect-period excerpt for the matching noninterpretation was similarly curtailed by the investigator; that is, the same length of time was allotted for it as for the interpretive member of the pair. These curtailed effect periods ranged in length from somewhat less than two minutes to somewhat less than five minutes.

WORD COUNTS

From this point in the study, only the excerpts of the hours were worked with; that is, each selected interpretation plus its five-minute effect period and each selected noninterpretation plus its five-minute effect period were used.

Since word counts had been selected as one index of verbal activity, the number of words in each remark by the therapist and by the patient was tallied. Rules for such word counts were minimal; contractions were counted as two words: meaningless vocalizations were counted as no words; if enough of a word was enunciated to be understood, it was counted; and repeated or stuttered words were counted the number of times they occurred. Here, as with the timings, more attention was given to consistency than to very fine precision.

When timings and word counts had been recorded, the preliminary preparation of the data was complete. These measures were tabulated in several ways, and a number of other ratings and classifications were made which will be discussed specifically in subsequent sections.

---

[7] To determine reliability, independent timings by staff members of the Psychotherapy Project were compared. Computation based on a sequence of 76 statements yielded a Pearson r of .99. A similar procedure for word counts, based on 22 statements, also yielded a Pearson r of .99.

[8] Case 2, hours 100, 148, 157, 288; Case 4, hours 12, 18, 19, 25, 29, 33.

3

SOME CHARACTERISTICS OF THE ACTIVITY OF THERAPISTS

The independent variables of this research were selected and classified on the basis of their interpretive or noninterpretive content. In working with them it became apparent that certain other characteristics of these interventions also merited consideration. In addition, the question arose whether additional verbalizations of therapists would be substantially different after they had made an interpretation. That is, would their activity be different in interpretation and noninterpretation effect periods? To provide a more complete picture of the activity of therapists, data were systematically collected on the following:

Number of words in intervention. The total number of words in each selected interpretation and noninterpretation, regardless of whether such intervention consisted of one or more than one numbered therapist statement, was tallied. (Recall that the number of therapist *statements* in the noninterpretation was controlled by the number of therapist statements in the interpretation.)

Number of therapist words in effect period. The total number of words in all therapist statements during each effect period was tallied.

Incidence of interventions that end in an inquiry. Interpretations and noninterpretations were divided into those that ended in a declarative sentence and those that ended in an interrogative sentence. This classification was made in view of a rather obvious tendency of the material to divide itself along these lines, and because of theoretical considerations that the form of the therapist's "input" influences the response by the patient (see, for example, Colby, 1961). In some instances, an intervention consisting

28

of several explanatory, declarative sentences ended in a direct question. Such interventions were classified as ending in an inquiry, as were those in which the question was conveyed by inflection: e.g., "You feel it would be humiliating for her?"

Incidence of effect periods containing interpretations. If this study had been set up as an experimental paradigm of psychotherapy, the therapist would have said nothing more in the five minutes following a selected therapist intervention, so an "uncontaminated" effect period would have been obtained. This study is based on actual therapy hours, however, and since analysts talk as they choose rather than on a prearranged schedule, such unmixed effect periods may or may not occur. To get some indication of the incidence of interpretations in effect periods, all effect-period material was read by the senior author. She then divided it into effect periods containing one or more interpretations, and those containing no interpretations.

STATISTICAL PROCEDURES

The preceding data were machine processed to yield specified sums, means, sigmas, correlations, and t or chi-square values. For the word-count variables, differences between interpretations and noninterpretations were tested by a t-test formula for correlated means, since the data for the two experimental conditions had been drawn from the same psychotherapy hours. For the two variables involving dichotomous categorization and total incidence, chi-square corrected for small frequencies was used.

RESULTS AND DISCUSSION

Information about the activity of therapists is presented in Table 2. There is a conspicuous difference between the mean length of interpretations and that of noninterpretations: interpretations were, on the average, more than five times as long. There is no doubt that interpretations consist of more words than do noninterpretations. Indeed, the test of statistical significance only confirms what had been evident in the gathering of the data. Appar-

TABLE 2

DIFFERENCES IN THE ACTIVITY OF THERAPISTS IN RELATION
TO INTERPRETATIONS AND NONINTERPRETATIONS

Variable	Interpretations (N = 60)	Noninterpretations (N = 60)	t or χ^2	p[a]
Mean number of words in intervention	176.0	31.3	8.35	<.001
Mean number of therapist words in effect period following intervention	109.6	92.7	1.12	ns
Total number of interventions that end in an inquiry	9 (15.0%)	25 (41.7%)	9.23	<.005
Total number of effect periods containing interpretations	19 (31.7%)	10 (16.7%)	2.91	<.10

[a]Based on t (two-tailed tests), or χ^2, corrected for small frequencies.

ently, the greater length of interpretations has to be considered as one of the inevitable realities of the psychoanalytically oriented psychotherapy process.

Interpretations were not only longer than noninterpretations, they were less frequently phrased as questions. Only 15% of the interpretations in this study ended in an inquiry, whereas almost 42% of the noninterpretations were stated in the interrogative. From these data, it is clear that interpretations were sometimes presented in question form, but that other therapist interventions were more frequently phrased interrogatively. Certainly, in clinical practice interpretations tend to be declarations by the therapist, even when they are tentatively or cautiously put forward. Also, in this context, one immediately thinks of the many noninterpretations that are directive or nondirective probes.

Does the marked difference in amount of therapist verbal activity continue during the five-minute periods following interpretations and noninterpretations? According to our data, the answer is no. Table 2 indicates that in interpretation effect periods therapists averaged 110 words. In noninterpretation effect periods they averaged 93 words. This difference is relatively small and not statistically significant. Both in this comparison and on an absolute basis, then, therapists did not continue to talk at exceptional length after they had made their interpretations. They slowed down to a level of activity which was more characteristic of the psychotherapeutic session in general and may be described as one of relative passivity. It is noteworthy that approximately 100 words per five minutes leaves a large portion of the designated effect periods available for patients to utilize.

Therapists did, however, show a tendency ($p < .10$) to interpret more after interpretations than after noninterpretations. That is, interpretations were followed by interpretations almost twice as often as noninterpretations were followed by interpretations. But at best, the incidence of interpretations in effect periods was not high.

The finding that only about a third of interpretation effect periods had interpretations in them is unexpected. One might well anticipate that an interpretation would usually be followed by further amplification and repetition. Nor can the modest difference between postinterpretation and postnoninterpretation incidence be readily explained by methodological factors. In the selection of interpretations only the essential content of the interpretation was included; accordingly, there would still be opportunity for minor amplifications and repetitions of that interpretation to appear in the effect period following it. Furthermore, since interpretations theoretically are expected to occur more frequently later in an hour than early, it is possible that the method of always selecting them slightly further along in the hour than noninterpretations would favor additional interpretations. Thus, on a *strictly* temporal basis, there should be more interpretations in the five minutes following the selected interpretations. And indeed there were, but not impressively so. The data probably are best taken to indicate that even psychoanalytically oriented psychotherapists are cautious in their use of interpretations. As we already know, the total incidence of interpretations of moderate or greater scope is not great. The findings here suggest that even when the therapist does interpret, he does not continue to do so with marked persistence. Once he has made his point, he is more likely than not to switch to other types of intervention.

Although there is a tendency to interpret more following interpretations, there is no similar (statistical) tendency for therapists
to talk more in such periods. But this seems to be inconsistent
with our earlier finding that interpretations are so much longer
than noninterpretations. The explanation for the apparent contra-
diction is twofold. Since postinterpretation interpretations may be
repetitions or minor expansions of earlier formulations, they are
likely to be shorter than interpretations that occur elsewhere. Also, therapists did average a few more words after interpretations,
so the difference, while not significant, was at least in the anticipated direction.

The preceding findings concern therapists as a group and, presumably, as a relatively homogeneous group. But were they homogeneous? Without presenting individual cases in detail, we can nevertheless cite some relevant data.[1] Thus, we found that every one
of our therapists averaged more words in his interpretations than
in his noninterpretations, and that each therapist also used the
question form less frequently in his interpretations than in his
noninterpretations. Even though only the differences in the length
of interpretations were statistically significant ($p < .01$ in all four t
tests), our therapists are clearly similar in both of these reports.

Were there also similarities among individual therapists with regard to effect-period activity? While the group finding discussed
earlier indicated that therapists did not significantly differ in the
amount of their postinterpretation and postnoninterpretation activity, individual therapists varied: two talked more after interpretations, and two talked less. In absolute numbers of words, therapists could be placed on a continuum: Therapist 4 talked considerably more after interpretations than after noninterpretations
($p < .05$), Therapist 2 somewhat more after interpretations, Therapist 1 a trifle less, and Therapist 3 somewhat less ($p < .05$). Earlier
we also showed that the group tendency was to interpret more
following interpretations, but individually only Therapist 2
($p < .005$) and Therapist 3 did so. The other two therapists did
not, but the difference was very slight: following interpretations
only one less of the effect periods contained interpretations. Individually considered, then, therapists were quite idiosyncratic in

---

[1] For more detailed data on individual therapists, see Levitov (1965).

their effect-period verbalization and somewhat so in their additional use of interpretations.

It is apparent, from these and other data, that there were both consistencies and variations among our therapists. It may also be noted here that, in classifying individual cases from a psychoanalytic point of view, Therapist 2 was considered the most orthodox practitioner in our group and Therapist 3 the least.

Let us return to the strongest finding in this chapter—that interpretations are much longer than noninterpretations. Even though this may be so typical of interpretations as to be an indisputable "given" of psychoanalytically oriented psychotherapy, it is indeed a striking characteristic. It provokes some thought, including a critical question—for the psychoanalytically oriented—concerning the paramount importance of interpretive *content.* To what extent is the length of the intervention, rather than its type, the crucial factor in determining patient reactions to it? That is, would any comparably long interventions have the same effects on patients as do interpretations? Is the emphasis on correctness, timing, congruence with theory, depth, logical linkages, etc.—all of which are of serious import to the analyst—essentially irrelevant as far as the patient is concerned? Are his differential responses to interpretations, if there are any, responses to the obvious time and interest that the therapist has invested in the interpretation, not to its actual content?

Questions such as these are unanswerable in the present study. To determine the relative importance of length per se would require examination of patient reactions to noninterpretations of a length comparable to that of interpretations. But, for the cases and methodology of this study, such comparable noninterpretations were quite scarce, and did not exist at all for comprehensive interpretations. And, if this sample of cases is representative of psychoanalytically oriented therapies with neurotic patients and experienced analysts, one would also be unlikely to find many relatively long noninterpretations in other cases. The noninterpretations that come closest to interpretations in length are probably either those that are quite close to interpretations in content, or those that consist of some other type of information-giving. As we shall see later, our "close" noninterpretations were, on the average, about half as long as our moderate interpretations, and less than a fifth as long as our comprehensive interpretations. We have no systematic data on the quite long noninterpretive explanations or recommendations that therapists may give with regard to such topics as therapy procedures, financial arrangements, sexual information, behavior toward other family members, etc. It is our impression, however, that while such relatively long interventions may occur from time to time in individual, long-term, psychoanalytically oriented psychotherapy, they are more characteristic of other types of therapy.

Since comparably long noninterpretations are so infrequent, an opposite research approach might be feasible, despite marked difficulties in validation. One might locate "comparably short" interpretations through the use of sound recordings and movies. Definitional criteria different from those of the present study would be necessary. For example, implied interpretations and interpretations conveyed partly by vocal inflections and gestures of the therapist might be sampled. Probably a more desirable strategy would be to shift the problem from the length of selected interventions to the total amount of therapist activity in a given hour. A comparison of hours with similar total amounts of therapist verbalization but dissimilar amounts of interpretation might well be a more meaningful, practical, and nonatomistic way of isolating the importance of content in psychoanalytically oriented therapy. (But see the earlier discussion on control of factors peculiar or unique to a given hour.)

To conclude this chapter, let us summarize the empirical findings that have been presented. Therapists' interpretations are longer than their noninterpretations, and are less often expressed as questions than are noninterpretations. While the amount of therapist verbalization in the two types of effect periods is not significantly different, the content tends to be more interpretive in interpretation effect periods. These findings characterize therapists as a group, but they frequently do not hold for individual therapists.

4

FORM OF PATIENT MATERIAL FOLLOWING INTERPRETATIONS AND NONINTERPRETATIONS

One major focus of the present research is on certain form qualities assumed to be indicative of the responsiveness and productivity of patients. This chapter centers on the following questions: Do patients react more quickly to interpretations or to noninterpretations? Do they talk more in the five-minute periods after interpretations than in comparable postnoninterpretation periods? Which kind of intervention is followed by more silence?

To answer these questions, data on several characteristics were selected from the timings and word counts that had already been made. Some of these were obviously highly related, e.g., percentage of effect period patient talks and number of patient words in effect period.[1] Nevertheless, each of the following variables was judged to be of interest in itself.

Patient's reaction time. This was defined as the interval of time between the end of the selected intervention and the beginning of the response by the patient. When an intervention encompassed several numbered therapist remarks, i.e., when it was a sequence, the reaction time was measured from the end of the sequence.

Number of patient words in effect period. The total number of words in all patient statements during a given effect period was counted. Patient verbalizations that occurred within the interven-

---

[1] All of the form variables were intercorrelated (Pearson r's) in the IBM processing of the data. While the resulting correlation matrices are not presented in this study, they are briefly mentioned in Levitov (1965) and are the basis for a factor-analytic study now in preparation.

tion period were not included in this total; this was necessary so that the five-minute base would be constant.

Percentage of effect period patient talks. The total duration of all patient statements during a given effect period was measured. This total time was then converted into a percentage of five minutes (or less where appropriate, i.e., for curtailed effect periods).

Percentage of available effect period patient talks. The five-minute effect periods in this study were composed of "time therapist talks," "time patient talks," and "silence." Since the patient could not talk during the time the therapist was talking (a few simultaneous comments did occur, but were so brief that their duration was ignored), this part of the effect period was considered unavailable to the patient. Such "unavailable time" could vary from therapist to therapist, and from one part of an hour to another, and so make certain experimental findings difficult to interpret. For example, a patient might talk less after interpretations because less of the effect period was actually available to him. The present measure was derived in order to have a measure of the patient's verbal activity, regardless of how active the therapist was. It was computed by converting the total duration of all patient statements during a given effect period into a percentage of the total amount of time available to the patient in that effect period (total effect-period time minus therapist time).

Percentage of effect-period (patient) silence. Silence was defined as that part of the effect period during which no one was talking, excluding pauses of less than 10 seconds within either therapist or patient statements. All pauses between numbered therapist and patient statements were counted as silence. To obtain the present variable, the total duration of all silences during a given effect period was converted into a percentage of five minutes (or less where appropriate).

The assumption made in this study that silence is a function of the patient is, of course, an oversimplification. In a dyadic interchange, silence must necessarily be a function of both participants. Nevertheless, the theoretical model of a patient who should be free-associating whenever the therapist is not talking does imply that the amount of silence is regulated by the patient. Accordingly, silence is identified here as a patient variable, although it could be listed either as a joint therapist-patient variable or merely as silence without reference to its source. Furthermore, since it is treated as part of the "time available to the patient" it also seems more consistent to consider it as a patient variable here.[2]

STATISTICAL PROCEDURES

Means, sigmas, and correlations for the preceding five form variables were used to test the differences predicted in Hypotheses 1, 2, and 3. Since the data for the interpretation and noninterpretation conditions were drawn from the same psychotherapy hours, a t-test formula that took into account the correlation between paired observations was used. (In general, these correlations tended to be low and positive, so the standard error of the difference was only slightly smaller than it would have been if pairing had not been made.)

RESULTS AND DISCUSSION

Differences in the form of patient material following interpretations and noninterpretations are indicated in Table 3, which lists postinterpretation means, postnoninterpretation means, and t values and their probabilities.

Since all of the results indicated in Table 3 are statistically significant, it is obvious that interpretations elicit responses that are quantitatively different from responses to other therapist interventions. The first differential finding pertains to how quickly patients respond to interventions. While all reaction times were relatively brief, the mean reaction time to interpretations was approximately twice as long as it was to noninterpretations. Obviously, there is generally a longer latency in reacting to interpretations than to noninterpretations. Hypothesis 1, which predicts differences in reaction times of patients under the two experimental conditions, is therefore confirmed.

---

[2] Because of the design of this study, silence included even the brief one- or two-second intervals between some therapist and patient statements. Therefore, it encompassed some time that was not genuinely usable by the patient. From this point of view, silence and therefore "time available to the patient" were slightly inflated measures. However, the slight increments involved were assumed to be the same for both interpretation and noninterpretation effect periods.

TABLE 3

DIFFERENCES IN FORM OF PATIENT MATERIAL FOLLOWING
INTERPRETATIONS AND NONINTERPRETATIONS

Variable	Mean Following Interpretations ($N = 60$)	Mean Following Noninterpretations ($N = 60$)	t[a]	p[b]
Patient's reaction time (seconds)	8.8	4.0	2.56	<.02
Number of patient words in effect period	456.4	538.9	-2.40	<.02
Percentage of effect period patient talks	63.8	71.9	-2.88[c]	<.01
Percentage of available effect period patient talks	73.3	81.1	-2.37[c]	<.025
Percentage of effect period (patient) silence	22.5	16.3	2.98[c]	<.01

[a]Minus signs indicate noninterpretations followed by greater amount of specified variable.

[b]Probabilities based on t (two-tailed test).

[c]Based on arc-sine transformed data.

Three of the variables in Table 3 corroborate each other closely in their information concerning the amount of verbal activity of patients. Clearly, patients use fewer words and spend less time talking following interpretations than following noninterpretations. They are verbally active during less of the interpretation effect period both in absolute terms (as a percentage of the effect period) and when allowance has been made for their therapists' effect-period activity (as a percentage of the *available* effect period). Accordingly, Hypothesis 2, which predicts differences in patient verbal activity under the two experimental conditions, is confirmed.

It is of interest to note the activity level of patients regardless of whether a postinterpretation or postnoninterpretation period was involved. Patients averaged approximately 1,000 words in 10 minutes (five-minute postinterpretation effect period plus five-minute postnoninterpretation effect period). It will be recalled that therapists averaged approximately 200 words per 10 minutes when they were not making their "best" interpretations. Thus, patients talked about five times as much as their therapists did. While pertinent data from other researches are sparse, quite direct comparisons can be made with one study. Lennard and Bernstein (1960), who worked with other units of verbal output, found their "patients averaged about four times as much verbal material as the therapists" (p. 83). In view of the fact that the 10-minute periods referred to here do not include certain sections of the hour with high therapist activity (the most comprehensive interpretation in the hour), the findings from the two studies appear to be quite similar.

We have just indicated that patients talk less after interpretations than after noninterpretations. However, in an earlier chapter we showed that the average numbers of therapist words in both kinds of postintervention periods were not markedly different. Does it therefore follow that silence increased after interpretations? The final item in Table 3 indicates more silence after interpretations (approximately 22%) than after noninterpretations (approximately 16%). Hypothesis 3, which is relevant to patient silence, is confirmed. These data also may be considered in relation to some of the within-session findings reported by Lennard and Bernstein (1960, p. 80). They found that their high informational specificity category—a category that would include interpretations as defined in the present study—increased from the first third to the second third of psychotherapy sessions and then diminished. Average duration of silence increased from the first to the second to the last third of such sessions. Thus, the upsurge in informational specificity partially coincided with an upsurge in silence. While the variables in point can be compared only broadly, there does seem to be some agreement between the two studies on the association between interpretive material and silence. In contrast, our findings do not agree with those reported by Auld and White (1959) in a study that again permits only approximate comparison. Their data indicated about the same amounts of silence immediately after interpretations and after noninterpretive interventions by the therapist.

Before discussing the several findings of this chapter more generally, let us make two digressions. First, we shall consider an artifact of the effect-period material that might have influenced our
findings. It will be recalled that some of the effect periods in this
study were less than five minutes long. To determine whether this
unavoidable condition resulted in essentially dissimilar samples, all
form qualities that were studied were divided into two groups—
those from complete effect periods ($N = 50$) and those from curtailed ones ($N = 10$). Differences between these two subgroups
were computed separately for postinterpretation material and
postnoninterpretation material, using t tests for uncorrelated
means.

Only one variable was generally and significantly influenced by
the length of the effect period. Following interpretations the mean
number of patient words was 496 for complete effect periods and
258 for curtailed effect periods ($p < .001$). Following noninterpretations the mean number of patient words was 582 for complete
effect periods and 323 for curtailed effect periods ($p < .001$). This
finding, that fewer patient words occurred in curtailed effect periods than in complete ones, is obviously reasonable. And since the
decrease was very similar for both experimental conditions, it was
not a source of bias in the interpretation and noninterpretation
comparisons of the larger study. In view of these results, curtailed
and noncurtailed effect-period data were not treated separately.

Second, we wish to note some individual case findings,[3] with the
caution that most of them are not statistically significant and,
therefore, can only suggest certain patterns. Nevertheless, it is of
interest that three of our four patients reacted similarly on each of
the form variables studied. That is, everyone except Patient 4
reacted more slowly to interpretations than to noninterpretations
and everyone except Patient 3 was consistently less active after
them ($p < .05$ in seven out of 20 tests).

To look more closely at Patient 3's deviance: she either showed
somewhat more activity after interpretations (number of words
and percent of effect period patient talks) or essentially similar
amounts of activity under both conditions (percent of available
effect period patient talks and percent of silence). These responses

---

[3] For more detailed data on individual patients, see Levitov (1965).

seem to be a function of her therapist's effect-period activity, rather than of his interpretations and noninterpretations per se. We have already indicated that Therapist 3 talked less after interpretations than after noninterpretations. We now see that when he talked less (in interpretation effect periods), his patient talked more; when he talked more (in noninterpretation effect periods), his patient talked less. However, in both kinds of effect periods the patient talked about 90% of the time available to her and was silent about 10% of the time. Apparently, then, Patient 3 was not responding differentially to the preceding interpretation or noninterpretation. Since we already know that the Case 3 interpretations were less distinctive than those from other cases, this finding is not surprising.

To return to the hypotheses relevant to the form qualities of patient reactions: no prediction was made about whether there would be more or less of a given characteristic after interpretations than after noninterpretations. Nor was any one unifying point of view, covering all form variables, expressed. All of the findings cited in this chapter are consistent with the proposition that it is at least more complicated and probably more difficult to deal with interpretations than with noninterpretations. Explanations of this complexity derive both from relatively manifest and from more inferential considerations.

It has been emphasized that interpretations are longer than noninterpretations. One obvious explanation of the longer reaction times to interpretations is that the patient is waiting to be sure that the therapist has finished his formulation. Since an interpretation can continue for a number of sentences, it may not always be clear whether the therapist is merely hesitating before continuing, or whether he has completed his communication. Similarly, it is easier to recognize the ending of an interrogative sentence than that of a declarative one, and our data showed a preponderance of the latter in interpretations. A simple basis can also be suggested for the diminished patient verbalization and increased silence in the five minutes after interpretations. It may well be that, just after the interpretation, the patient is not only waiting but considers the therapist to have the initiative for some unknown period of time. In voicing his interpretation, the therapist has abandoned his passive role and has taken charge. It is his turn to talk, and unless he cues the patient—by a question, perhaps—the patient is not sure when his own turn will come again. Nor can the affective component of the patient's "waiting for more" be disregarded in this context. Most patients are eager to hear their therapists talk, regardless of whether they listen to their opinions. Since they characteristically want more from their therapists, they may well remain relatively inactive during postinterpretation periods.

It is probably more meaningful to explain the present findings on a different content basis. It seems logical that it would take longer to "process"—to receive, to think about, to understand, to integrate, and to react to—interventions that, by definition, present something new and may be quite intricate. In Chapter 5 it will be shown that interpretations elicit greater arousal of certain affective and cognitive reactions than do noninterpretations. During the five minutes following such relatively impactful interventions, the patient may be too busy with his own thoughts to verbalize freely. If interpretation is the most powerful technique of the therapist, it should indeed deeply engage the inner attention of the patient, and this may well be at the expense of his verbal quickness and productiveness.

The findings presented in this chapter, then, confirm Hypotheses 1, 2, and 3. They show that patients respond more slowly to interpretations than to noninterpretations, and that they talk less in (are silent for more of) the five minutes after interpretations than in similar periods following noninterpretations.

5

CONTENT OF PATIENT MATERIAL FOLLOWING INTERPRETATIONS AND NONINTERPRETATIONS

The practicing clinician is relatively indifferent to such "petty" details of the behavior of patients as their reaction times or the number of words they speak. He is concerned with the broader affective and cognitive content that they are communicating. He wants to know, "What do patients really do immediately after interpretations that they don't do after noninterpretations?" Do they show relief, do they become more defensive, do they "fall apart," do they produce more transference-related material? This chapter presents procedures and findings concerned with such questions as these.

PREPARATION OF CONTENT SCALES

Fourteen content scales (Table 4) were devised to measure the reactions and communications of patients following interpretations and noninterpretations. Ratings based on these scales were used to test Hypotheses 4 through 17. The scales were briefly identified in psychoanalytic terms, often without precise definitions. It was assumed that concepts such as deeper-level material, ego dysfunctioning, and resistance were part of the working terminology used by psychoanalytically oriented therapists and would therefore be meaningful to them. The scales and their descriptions were incorporated into a rating form with space for checking the amount of each variable as "none," "minimal," "some," or "much." A four-point scale rather than a five- or seven-point scale

TABLE 4

DESCRIPTION OF 14 CONTENT SCALES AND INTRACLASS CORRELATION
COEFFICIENTS BETWEEN RATINGS OF JUDGES C AND D

Relevant Hypothesis		Intraclass Correlation[a]	p
4	*Presence of affect:* Patient is expressing or discharging affect.	.28	$<.001$
5	*Anxiety:* Patient manifests anxiety, fear; feels threatened and upset.	.11	*ns*
6	*Anger, hostility, or aggression:* Patient manifests anger, hostility, or aggression.	.52	$<.001$
7	*Depression:* Patient manifests depression, morbid or dysphoric affect.	.32	$<.001$
8	*Pleasant affect:* Patient manifests relief, gratification, reassurance, pleasant affect.	.21	$<.025$
9	*Surprise:* Patient manifests surprise, startle.	.30	$<.001$
10	*Ego dysfunctioning:* Patient manifests disruption, marked confusion, inability to function, ego disorganization.	.04	*ns*
11	*Symptomatology:* Patient manifests alterations in symptoms or unmistakable aggravation of symptoms.	.13	*ns*
12	*Communication of conscious-level material:* Patient is communicating relatively factual, conscious-level material. He is reporting objectively, giving information, stating problems, describing events, etc.	.35	$<.001$
13	*Communication of deeper-level material:* Patient is communicating relatively subjective, deeper-level material. He is dealing with inner felt experience, searching self actively, observing inner feelings and reactions.	.23	$< .01$

14	*Blocking of associations*: Patient manifests blocking in associations or difficulty in producing associations.	.13	*ns*
15	*Defensive and oppositional associations*: Patient's associations are generally defensive or oppositional in relation to what has apparently been communicated to him. He expresses denial, repudiation, exaggerated doubt, or hostility to the therapist as manifestations of resistance. He tries to distort, evade, or change the subject.	.46	$< .001$
16	*Understanding and insight*: Patient shows understanding or insight in regard to what has apparently been communicated to him. This category includes both "simple" understanding (Yes, I can understand that) and insight (I would not have thought of that but I recognize it now).	.37	$< .001$
17	*Transference-related material*: Patient is apparently dealing with transference-related material.	.52	$< .001$

[a]Correlations based on $N = 120$.

was used because preliminary experience with this type of material indicated that finer discriminations had more face validity than actual validity.

PREPARATION OF EXPERIMENTAL DATA

The excerpts from the psychotherapy hours were coded before rating. All remarks by the therapist, beginning with the first word of the interpretation or noninterpretation, were eliminated from the transcripts and replaced by dashes; identifications of cases, pages, and patient remarks were replaced by new coded identifications, and anything else, such as length of material deleted, that might cue a reader about whether he was dealing with an interpretation portion of material, was removed.

We indicated earlier that some of the selected interventions consisted of a sequence of therapist statements. The patient remarks that occurred between the parts of such interventions were retained in the excerpts given to the judges to rate. (They were not included in the measurement of form qualities.) Because of the study design, the same number of such intervening patient statements occurred for a given interpretation excerpt and its paired noninterpretation. The rationale for retaining these intervention-period remarks was that certain content qualities that were being judged—such as surprise—might be more clearly manifested after the first part of a formulation by the therapist than after it was completed.

RATING PROCEDURE

On the assumption that maximally valid ratings would best be obtained from psychoanalytically oriented clinicians, two psychoanalysts were asked to participate in this research. They were not informed of its exact purposes. They were told that they would be dealing with brief portions of patient material from actual but anonymous psychotherapy hours, that they would be judging variables that usually interest psychotherapists, and that they would be rating such variables on continua that had been divided into four categories. After each judge agreed to rate independently the 120 coded, randomized psychotherapy excerpts, he was given the material and rating forms as well as additional relevant instructions.

The judges chosen were experienced as clinicians, not as raters. Nevertheless, they were not given preliminary training in rating the excerpts, for several reasons. Even though they would be working with limited portions of material, the qualitative judgments that were explicitly called for in the study resemble those that analysts are presumed to make implicitly in clinical practice. Moreover, since the judges were graduates of the same psychoanalytic institute, it was hoped that they would be relatively similar in judging variables emphasized in the theory of psychotherapy they shared.

Also, since both judges had themselves been analyzed, it was thought that they would be able to "correct for" many of the biasing internal cues that may be major determinants in ratings of psychotherapy material. A final consideration was the limited amount of time the judges could give to this task. As it was, the actual rating was relatively time-consuming—Judge C spent approximately eight hours on the task, Judge D approximately 10.

When the ratings were completed, numerical scores of 0 to 3 were assigned to the four categories for each scale. Each judge's ratings and their combined ratings for every scale were then tabulated separately for interpretation and (paired) noninterpretation excerpts. For illustrative purposes, two rated excerpts of patient material are presented as Appendix C.

Reliability of Ratings

To determine the reliability of these ratings, intraclass correlation coefficients (R) were computed between Judge C and Judge D on each of the 14 content scales. These were based on all the material that was rated $(N = 120)$. The formula that was chosen utilized a two-way classification of data so that variance due to differences in judge means (or bias) was partialed out (Haggard, 1958, p. 38). Pearson r's were also computed, but since they were essentially the same as the intraclass R's, they will not be specifically referred to.

The results of these computations are presented in Table 4. For 10 out of 14 scales, the intraclass correlation coefficients were statistically significant, but low to moderate. That is, consistency did exist between the ratings of the two judges; the coefficients were highly stable but relatively small. That the correlations tended to be low may be due not only to the usual difficulties of agreement on highly inferential material, but also to the limited ranges worked with. Of further relevance here is the rating procedure for each content scale. Within some of the five-minute excerpts a given variable might sometimes have been "minimal" and sometimes "much." However, since the raters had been instructed to give only one rating, they may well have checked the "some" category in such instances. In effect, this would further shrink the scales and lower correlation coefficients. Higher correlations might have been obtained if judges had been instructed differently—for example, to rate each excerpt upward, according to the highest amount of a particular variable manifested at any time within a given excerpt. In addition to these points, it seems likely that the choice of analysts because of validity considerations also entailed some sacrifice of the reliability that is obtainable with experienced raters.

While the reliability correlations varied considerably, the most substantial ones occurred in connection with the patient's communications rather than his other responses, except for the *Anger, hostility, or aggression* scale ($R = .52$). The correlations on four scales—*Anxiety, Ego dysfunctioning, Blocking of associations*, and *Symptomatology*—were too low to be statistically significant. The finding that judges could agree no better than chance in rating anxiety was disappointing in view of the pronounced theoretical importance of this concept in psychotherapy. Their lack of agreement on *Ego dysfunctioning* may be due to the broadness and lack of specificity of this term. *Blocking*, which may be considered as one aspect of ego dysfunctioning, is possibly difficult to rate because it involves judging something partially by its absence. Finally, the lack of agreement on *Symptomatology* may be related to its rare incidence in the material. Because these four scales were not reliably rated, they were eliminated from the study.

FURTHER STATISTICAL PROCEDURES

Since the interjudge reliabilities for the 10 remaining scales were relatively low, even though statistically significant, we treated the ratings of each judge separately, as well as their combined (averaged) ratings, in testing the content hypotheses of the study. Thus, specified means, sigmas, correlations, and t tests for differences between paired data were obtained for Judge C, for Judge D, and for Judges C and D. Inasmuch as no "true" rating for the content material existed, the averaged rating of the two judges was considered the "best" rating. The data processing also included preparation of intercorrelation matrices to indicate relationships among the content scales. In the present study, these correlations were used as an occasional aid in interpreting certain other results, and are therefore referred to only briefly.

RESULTS AND DISCUSSION

Mean ratings for, and differences in, the content of patient material following interpretations and noninterpretations are indicated in Table 5. It will be recalled that our scale categories ranged from 0 for "none" to 3 for "much." Note also that t-test probabilities are based on one-tailed regions of significance because of the nature of the content hypotheses.

The mean ratings on all but two scales fell within the "minimum" to "some" range. For *Surprise* and *Pleasant affect*, most of the mean ratings fell below this range. The highest ratings in the data were on *Presence of affect, Communication of conscious-level material*, and *Communication of deeper-level material*, but even these were not outstandingly high. It is clear that the judges of the patient material used the "much" rating sparingly. Apparently, the immediate effects of interventions by therapists are not strong and dramatic, or at least are not judged to be strongly and dramatically manifested. Of course, this conclusion is limited to judgments based on typescripts of psychotherapy material.

In this general context, we may note that the present ratings were obviously made on much less material than is customarily available in clinical practice. In the latter, therapists have broader knowledge about their patients, remember their previous reactions, see and hear their current ones, spend many hours with them, know what kinds of interventions they themselves have made, etc. In view of the different criteria for judgment that are involved, the magnitude of patient reactions reported here may well be considerably different from (smaller than) that reported in clinical practice. However, this study attempts to get at differences between interpretations and noninterpretations per se—as two distinct types of intervention—and from this point of view therapists' memories, etc., may represent "contaminating" knowledge.

For the combined mean ratings of the two judges, statistically significant differences between interpretation and noninterpretation excerpts were found on four scales: *Defensive and oppositional associations* ($p < .025$), *Transference-related material* ($p < .05$), *Presence of affect* ($p < .05$), and *Understanding and insight* ($p < .025$). Unfortunately, in none of these instances did

TABLE 5

DIFFERENCES IN CONTENT OF PATIENT MATERIAL FOLLOWING
INTERPRETATIONS AND NONINTERPRETATIONS

Judge	Mean Rating Following Interpretations ($N = 60$)	Mean Rating Following Noninterpretations ($N = 60$)	t^a	p^b
I. Scales for Which Some Differences Were Significant				
Defensive and oppositional associations				
Judge C	1.32	0.95	2.30	$<.025$
Judge D	0.92	0.72	1.24	$< .15$
Judges C and D	1.11	0.83	2.08	$<.025$
Transference-related material				
Judge C	0.95	0.58	2.16	$<.025$
Judge D	1.08	0.92	1.04	$<.15+$
Judges C and D	1.02	0.75	1.92	$< .05$
Presence of affect				
Judge C	2.03	1.90	1.30	$< .10$
Judge D	1.87	1.68	1.59	$< .10$
Judges C and D	1.95	1.79	1.82	$< .05$
Understanding and insight				
Judge C	1.05	0.95	0.64	ns
Judge D	1.38	0.92	3.01	$<.005$
Judges C and D	1.22	0.93	2.22	$<.025$
Communication of conscious-level material				
Judge C	1.75	1.73	0.17	ns
Judge D	1.45	1.68	-2.03	$<.025$
Judges C and D	1.60	1.71	-1.23	$< .15$
II. Scales for Which Some Differences Approached Significance				
Communication of deeper-level material				
Judge C	1.92	1.78	1.43	$< .10$
Judge D	1.93	1.87	0.45	ns
Judges C and D	1.92	1.82	0.99	$< .20$

Depression

Judge C	0.98	1.13	-1.38	< .10
Judge D	0.88	0.83	0.38	ns
Judges C and D	0.93	0.98	-0.50	ns

III. Scales for Which Differences Were Not Significant

Pleasant affect

Judge C	0.37	0.47	-0.77	ns
Judge D	0.52	0.62	-0.83	ns
Judges C and D	0.44	0.54	-1.04	< .20

Surprise

Judge C	0.20	0.32	-1.00	< .20
Judge D	0.52	0.43	0.70	ns
Judges C and D	0.36	0.38	-0.17	ns

Anger, hostility, or aggression

Judge C	1.10	1.23	-0.93	< .20
Judge D	1.17	1.22	-0.28	ns
Judges C and D	1.13	1.22	-0.66	ns

[a]Minus signs indicate noninterpretations followed by greater amount of specified variable.

[b]Probabilities based on t (one-tailed test).

the significant findings for each judge coincide when their ratings were considered separately. That is, Judge C's ratings yielded significant differences between the two experimental conditions on some scales, and Judge D's yielded significant differences in connection with other scales.

The combined mean rating for *Defensive and oppositional associations* was 1.11 following interpretations and 0.83 following noninterpretations. Similar decreases were found for both judges individually. Earlier, a moderate reliability had been found between the ratings of the two judges ($R = .46$) on this scale. If one considers together the high stability of that moderate relationship, the parallel tendencies in the t tests, and the t-test probabilities, the conclusion that there are more *Defensive and oppositional associations* after interpretations than after noninterpretations is adequately supported. Accordingly, Hypothesis 15 is confirmed.

The combined mean rating for *Transference-related material* was 1.02 following interpretations and 0.75 following noninterpretations. Again, similar decreases were found for both judges individually. Since the correlation coefficient between the two judges ($R = .52$) was again moderate and highly stable, the same considerations apply here as previously cited. The conclusion that more *Transference-related material* is dealt with after interpretations is adequately supported, and Hypothesis 17 is confirmed.

The combined mean rating for *Presence of affect* was 1.95 following interpretations and 1.79 following noninterpretations. For both judges individually parallel decreases from the former to the latter conditions were found. Earlier, a low reliability coefficient ($R = .28$) was found between the ratings of the two judges on this scale. Despite this low relationship between the two sets of ratings, each judge separately tended ($p < .10$) to find more affect after interpretations than after noninterpretations. And since for their combined ratings this difference between the two conditions was significant, the data permit the conclusion that more affect occurs in postinterpretation than in postnoninterpretation periods. Hypothesis 4 is confirmed.

The averaged rating for *Understanding and insight* was 1.22 following interpretations and 0.93 following noninterpretations. Both judges individually showed paralled decreases. But while this difference was highly significant for Judge D ($p < .005$), it was not significant for Judge C ($p < .30$). Furthermore, since the reliability between the judges on this scale was relatively low ($R = .37$), each judge apparently rated the material somewhat differently. The significant finding for the combined rating ($p < .025$) was highly influenced by the marked difference between the two conditions that was found for Judge D. However, the assumption was made earlier that the combined mean ratings would be considered the "best" ratings. Accordingly, the conclusion that there is more *Understanding and insight* after interpretations than after noninterpretations still warrants acceptance, despite what is known about the factors contributing to it. Therefore, Hypothesis 16 is confirmed.

For one judge only, differences were statistically significant, or nearly so, on three other content scales. Since these differences held for only one rater, they represent idiosyncratic findings that may, at best, be suggestive of more universal trends. Accordingly, Hypotheses 12, 13, and 7, which deal with *Communication of conscious-level material, Communication of deeper-level material,* and *Depression,* respectively, are considered to be not confirmed.

The final items in Table 5 indicate that there were no statistically significant or nearly significant differences on three scales: *Pleasant affect, Surprise,* and *Anger, hostility, or aggression.* It is on this basis that the relevant hypotheses, Hypotheses 8, 9, and 6, respectively, also are not confirmed.

Because of a lack of rater reliability, four hypotheses could not be tested. These were: Hypothesis 5 (*Anxiety*), Hypothesis 10 (*Ego dysfunctioning*), Hypothesis 11 (*Symptomatology*), and Hypothesis 14 (*Blocking*).

In evaluating the preceding results, an earlier form finding is relevant. We found less verbalization by patients and more silence following interpretations than following noninterpretations. Therefore, since patients did not talk as much after interpretations, there was less opportunity for certain kinds of associations to show up in the typescripts. Even though the patient material was rated globally, it is possible that the silence factor did influence the ratings. If it did, this factor would additionally reinforce the significant results that were obtained, since there was more of each specified quality following interpretations, despite a lesser opportunity for such a quality to be rated. Whether this reasoning is as applicable to *Defensive and oppositional associations* as it is to the other three scales on which clear differences were found between the two experimental conditions is open to question. *Defensive and oppositional associations* is a resistance scale, and inasmuch as fewer associations and more silence followed interpretations, this lack of patient material may have been judged as indicative of more defensiveness. Technically, however, such evaluations should have been made in connection with another resistance scale—*Blocking* (a scale later eliminated from the study).

From a different point of view, the influence of the amount of patient verbalization on the content ratings is irrelevant, since comparable portions of material were worked with for the two experimental conditions. If there was less verbalization in one experimental condition than in the other, then this difference is an authentic reflection of the nature of the psychotherapeutic process. Thus, this realistic characteristic may be accepted as a "given" in the present context.

To discuss other aspects of our data concerning *Defensive and oppositional associations*: The finding of more of such associations after interpretations is similar to findings reported from several, but not all, other studies of resistance. The extent to which identical qualities are being measured is, of course, highly problematical, but two studies are of direct relevance here. Speisman (1957) found that more "opposition" followed "deep" than "nondeep" interpretations. Since his "deep interpretations" correspond to our interpretations, and his "opposition category" of resistance is similar to the category we use, his results clearly agree with ours. This is not the case with the study of sequential dependencies reported by Auld and White (1959), who found no evidence that resistance was greater after interpretations.

Our *Defensive and oppositional associations* scale did not correlate highly[1] (*r*'s from .01 to .29) with any of the nine other content scales. We had looked particularly at *Anger* in this connection, since it may be the affective counterpart or foundation of defensiveness, and, indeed, there was some correlation (*r* = .29). However, our data showed no pronounced difference in the manifestation of *Anger, hostility, or aggression* under the two experimental conditions. Consequently, although interpretations elicited more defensive associations, we cannot say that they also elicited more anger.

Of equal moment with resistance in psychoanalytic theory is the concept of transference. Freud indicated that the analyses of resistance and transference were procedures that characterized psychoanalysis (Jones, 1946). If interpretation is the major vehicle for this analysis, then it should noticeably influence both of these phenomena in our sample. We have just shown that it does for our

---

[1] A correlation of .50 was designated as the cutoff point for considering a relationship high, since correlations lower than this represented quite small amounts of the variance (<.25) of one quality that could be predicted by, or attributed to, another quality.

equivalent of resistance, but we do not have as exact an equivalent for transference. In this study, the only scale relevant to the transference measured the extent to which patients seemed to be dealing with material related to it. Our data showed interpretations were followed by more *Transference-related material.* Since interpretations elicited more of such material, it seems reasonable to infer that they also had a greater influence than noninterpretations on the transference itself.

This chapter discusses transference-related material only as it relates to our major division between interpretations and noninterpretations. But a later unexpected finding bears mentioning here. When we looked at our comprehensive interpretations separately, we found that they did not elicit appreciably more transference-related material than noninterpretations. There was even a slight suggestion—clearly not beyond chance but in an unanticipated direction—that they might be the poorest elicitors of such material (mean rating of 0.50 for comprehensive interpretations, 0.75 for noninterpretations). Reasons for the relative ineffectiveness of comprehensive interpretations are discussed in Chapter 6. In this context, however, we can clearly particularize our general finding by indicating that patients deal with more transference-related material after moderate-limited interpretations than after noninterpretations.

The question of understanding and insight on the part of the patient is of concern in most theories of psychotherapy, although their role as a primary agent of change is in some dispute (Hobbs, 1962). Psychoanalytic theory postulates that insight precedes change, and that interpretation is the principal technique through which insight is effected. Our results corroborate this formulation in part in that they showed that more *Understanding and insight* followed interpretations than noninterpretations. We have no data pertaining to the relationship between understanding and change.

Since patients who discuss subjective, nonmanifest material frequently seem to be showing understanding, we looked at the relationship between these two scales. We found that the only high correlation among all the content scales was between *Understanding and insight* and *Communication of deeper-level material* ($r = .58$). The data provide some empirical support for the notion that these two behaviors tend to go together.

The confirmation of our hypothesis regarding understanding was not paralleled by confirmation of certain hypotheses concerning affects that would be suitable in this connection. A feeling of surprise in combination with the "aha" experience of sudden insight is often cited, but our *Understanding and insight* and *Surprise* scales were not highly correlated. *Pleasant affect* might well be expected to accompany *Understanding and insight*, but again, the correlation between our two scales was not high. Such data did not preclude the possibility that interpretations would be more effective than other interventions in eliciting these emotions. However, we found no marked differences in the amounts of either *Surprise* or *Pleasant affect* under the two experimental conditions.

Indeed, for none of the specifically described affects were significant differences found between the two experimental conditions. But when the type of affect was not specified, that is, when the rating called for *Presence of affect*, significantly more affect was judged to occur after interpretations than after noninterpretations. These results do not dovetail. The discrepancy is emphasized if one refers to the mean ratings for the several affects listed in Table 5. The table shows that it was the noninterpretations that were followed by slightly more *Anger, Pleasant affect, Surprise*, and *Depression.* While these differentials in favor of noninterpretations represent chance findings only, their similar direction is of interest. This, plus the "opposite" finding for *Presence of affect*, signals the possible importance for interpretations of some type of affect other than those measured.

One immediately speculates about the role of anxiety here, in view of its prominent position in psychic experience and psychotherapy theory. Our *Anxiety* ratings, it will be recalled, were not reliable and had to be eliminated from the study. This is particularly unfortunate, since, theoretically, anxiety is very likely to be the type of affect that increases after an interpretation.

One can also speculate about the increase in affects that are not readily identifiable, but imbue an interaction with a distinctive emotional atmosphere—perhaps dependency-related affects, or the complex of emotions associated with intimate disclosures, or excitement, or empathy. It may well be that the greater *Presence of affect* after interpretations is related to changes in phenomena such as these, rather than to changes in affects that can be more specifically identified.

We found that affect increased after interpretations; are there corroborative findings from other studies? Again, the closest comparison that can be made is with the work of Lennard and Bernstein (1960). They found that their "interpretation-redirection" category elicited high patient verbalization about affect for three of their four therapists. However, they also reported that "There appear to be no consistent trends among therapists with regard to which informational categories are most effective for the production of patient verbalization about affect" (p. 140). Since our interpretations were more effective than noninterpretations in eliciting affect, the two studies apparently disagree.

Four of the six hypotheses of the study that were not confirmed dealt with various types of affect. The other two pertained to communication of manifest and deep-level material by patients—interpretations, as contrasted to noninterpretations, did not elicit significantly less of the former or more of the latter. It may be noted that the mean ratings in Table 5 do show that interpretations, considered by themselves, were followed by a greater amount of deeper-level (1.92) than conscious-level material (1.60). But so were noninterpretations, although not to the same extent (1.82 for deeper-level and 1.71 for conscious-level material). The data indicating that interpretations are not significantly more effective in eliciting deeper-level associations are disappointing, both because of the important role ascribed to them by psychoanalytic theory and in view of the relatively high relationship between *Communication of deeper-level material* and *Understanding and insight* that was pointed out earlier.

To recapitulate, out of the total of 10 content hypotheses that were tested, four were confirmed and six were not. On the basis of these data, it is sound to infer that interpretations are relatively effective interventions in some respects, but are not particularly so in others. They are not omnipotent. The findings do not encourage the view that interpretations are "something extremely powerful whether for good or ill" (Strachey, 1934, p. 18).

But while this may be so for findings based on grouped data, perhaps it is the individual case that is the critical factor here. Clearly, some patients may be greatly influenced by interpretations, and others not. In view of this possibility, we looked at our four cases individually.

First, as a preliminary to other observations, we ascertained the reliability of ratings for each case. As might be anticipated, agreement between judges varied considerably across and within variables and patients. Despite this wide range, judges did agree more on certain reactions than others, and more on certain patients than on others. They were most consistent in evaluating *Anger, hostility, or aggression, Understanding and insight, Defensive and oppositional associations,* and *Transference-related material*, agreeing significantly on these scales in three out of four cases—but not always the same three ($p < .05$ based on Pearson r). In contrast, in none of the individual cases could the judges agree significantly in rating *Blocking* or *Anxiety*. Of the four patients, the judges saw Patient 4 most similarly. In rating him, they agreed beyond chance on approximately twice as many scales—nine—as they did in rating Patient 1, whom they were least successful in rating similarly. We can only speculate about why Patient 4 was rated most reliably: possibilities include the nature of his problem, the relative brevity of his therapy, and the fact that the patient was a male.

Second, we looked for differences in reactions to interpretations and noninterpretations within each case, using t tests. Partly because of the small Ns, most of these did not yield statistically significant results: there were 10 nonchance findings in 56 tests. Furthermore, only four of these 10 significant findings were based on reliable ratings. Thus our statistical evidence did not point to any great effectiveness of interpretations in the individual case.

Putting aside statistical considerations, we scanned our data to see which patients had the largest differences in affect, anger, etc., under the two experimental conditions. From this point of view, Patient 2 clearly led in differential reactions. Differences between interpretations and noninterpretations were larger for this case than for any other case on nine out of the 14 content variables. That is, Patient 2 showed greater differences in *Anxiety, Presence of affect, Ego dysfunctioning, Symptomatology, Communication of deeper-level material, Blocking of associations, Defensive and oppositional associations, Understanding and insight,* and *Pleasant affect* than did any other patient. In addition, in each instance except the last, reactions were more pronounced after interpretations than after noninterpretations. The exception, *Pleasant affect*, was greater after noninterpretations. Rather strikingly, then, Patient 2 was most greatly influenced by interpretations. This is of interest in the light of previous knowledge that Case 2 is the most orthodox case in our group. It may well be that the more classical the "input" in psychotherapy, the more classical the response.

Finally, we wanted to know to what extent our major positive findings concerning content were characteristic for each case. In four out of four cases we found more *Presence of affect, Defensive and oppositional associations,* and *Transference-related material* after interpretations than after noninterpretations. Although none of the values was statistically significant, these results were nicely consistent. Such consistency did not obtain for any of the other content responses that we measured. This included *Understanding and insight*, which, it will be recalled, was markedly greater after interpretations for our grouped data. Individually, however, only Patients 2 and 4 showed more *Understanding and insight* after interpretations. (We thought it was noteworthy, however, that for both of these patients the differences were significant—$p < .005$, $p < .05$ respectively—and based on reliable ratings.)

Our summary comments on separate cases must be tempered by the lack of reliability of much of our evidence. Nevertheless, it seems reasonably clear that interpretations tend to be consistently effective elicitors of a few patient reactions, but that their effectiveness in relation to other reactions depends to some extent on the particular case under consideration.

After this long digression into the individual cases, let us now discuss the six major content hypotheses that were not confirmed. It is perhaps superfluous to state that the hypothesized differences may indeed exist, but to locate them would require a finer scientific net than ours. Nevertheless, we wish to emphasize two methodological considerations. The first concerns the difficulty of determining particular affects from typescripts only. Our judges were able to rate four specific types of affects reliably enough for us to study them, but the reliability coefficients were not high. *Surprise* and *Pleasant affect* were judged to occur rarely in the patient material, but how can such affects be detected in typescripts unless patients talk about them directly? Clinically, we know that patients talk more readily about "negative" affects. Preferably, then, judgments of affect should be made from sound, and, optimally, from sound movies. Second, even though this study was directed at the immediate effects of interpretations, five-minute portions of therapy sessions may provide inadequate material for judging various reactions. Unfortunately, an optimal portion of time cannot be specified. Perhaps the best guideline would parallel clinical practice. For example, therapists gauge the affect of their patients after an interpretation both from their responses during the rest of the hour and from those at the beginning of the subsequent hour. Parenthetically, it may be added that these considerations also apply to the scales that were eliminated from the study. *Anxiety, Ego dysfunctioning, Symptomatology,* and *Blocking* may all be strongly cued by vocal inflections, facial expressions, gestures, movements, etc., and possibly could have been reliably rated had sound films and longer portions of material been used.

In concluding this chapter, we may refer to an earlier conclusion that it is more complicated to deal with interpretations than with noninterpretations. Here some of the content factors relevant to that increased complexity have been specified. We have shown that interpretations elicit more defensive and oppositional associations, more transference-related material, more understanding and insight, and more affect from patients than do noninterpretations. In these respects, which, it may be noted, are neither exclusively intellectual nor exclusively affective, interpretations clearly have the greater immediate impact. However, they do not appreciably differ from noninterpretations in regard to other cognitive and affective qualities that have been discussed.

6

DIFFERENCES BETWEEN COMPRE-
HENSIVE AND MODERATE-LIMITED
INTERPRETATIONS

The interpretations used in this research were classified as either comprehensive or moderate-limited in scope. In the more than 300 therapy hours that were read, a total of only 12 comprehensive interpretations could be found. Because of their rare occurrence and complex content, it seemed worthwhile to examine them in detail. Were these interventions also distinctive in form? Did patients react differently to comprehensive interpretations than they did to other kinds of interpretations—i.e., moderate-limited ones? If so, were the effects so distinctive as to suggest that these interventions had a special, and perhaps critical, role in the psychotherapy process? Was there evidence that comprehensive interpretations might prove to be the real agents of change in psychotherapy?

To provide information on such questions from the several variables of this study, all data were divided according to their association with either comprehensive or moderate-limited interpretations. Differences between groups were tested either by t, using a formula for independent means, or by chi-square. Out of a total of 19 comparisons, differences on two therapist variables, two patient form variables, and four patient content variables were statistically significant.

RESULTS AND DISCUSSION

In general, only our positive findings will be presented in detail. Two of the variables descriptive of therapist activity are graphed in

Figure 1. The mean length of comprehensive interpretations (349 words) was more than two-and-a-half times that of moderate-limited ones ($p < .001$);[1] following comprehensive interpretations therapists averaged more than twice as many words (192) as they did following moderate-limited ones ($p < .01$). Thus, therapists clearly talked more both while making comprehensive interpretations and in the effect periods following them. Furthermore, our data also showed a tendency ($p < .10$ based on χ^2) for therapists to interpret more after they made comprehensive interpretations. That is, while 58% of the effect periods following comprehensive

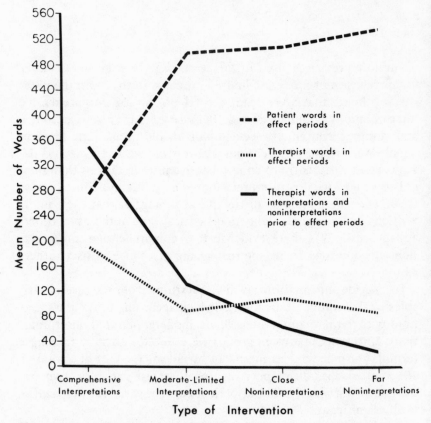

Figure 1 Mean Number of Words in Interpretations and Noninterpretations and in the Five-Minute Effect Periods following Them

[1] Unless otherwise indicated, ps for form variables are based on two-tailed t tests. Where mean percentages apply, ts are based on arc-sine transformations of the data.

interpretations contained interpretations, only 25% of the moderate-limited effect periods did.

Patients did not respond significantly differently to the two types of interpretations in their reaction times and in their silence, although both were greater after comprehensive interpretations. They did show significantly different responses in how much they talked. As indicated in Figure 1, the average number of patient words after comprehensive interpretations was 274, whereas after moderate-limited interpretations it was 502 ($p < .001$).[2] Similar results were yielded by a closely related comparison: patients talked about 50% of the time in effect periods following comprehensive interpretations, but about 67% of the time following moderate-limited ones ($p < .01$). Thus, patients were clearly less active after comprehensive interpretations. But was this merely because their therapists were talking more after such interpretations? To answer this question we considered only the available effect-period time (time remaining after therapist time was eliminated) and found that patients talked 63% of this time after comprehensive interpretations and 76% after moderate-limited ones. Although this difference did not reach statistical significance ($p < .15$), it was strong enough to indicate that the type of interpretation was of importance as an influence here. It is sound to infer that patients were less active after comprehensive interpretations partly because of the increased activity of their therapists after such interpretations, and partly because of the effect of comprehensive interpretations per se.

For purposes of comparison with comprehensive and moderate-limited interpretations, we also looked at close and far noninterpretations. However, only our therapist and form variables were divided according to this subclassification and tested for differences. It will be recalled that "close on the interpretive continu-

[2] Earlier it was shown that patients uttered fewer words during curtailed effect periods than in full effect periods. If such curtailed effect periods tended to follow comprehensive interpretations, the present finding might have no intrinsic relationship to comprehensive interpretations but, rather, might be only an artifact. However, only two of the 10 curtailed effect periods followed comprehensive interpretations. Furthermore, the average length of effect periods following comprehensive interpretations was four minutes and 37 seconds, and following moderate-limited ones it was four minutes and 42 seconds. In view of this similarity, the cited results cannot be ascribed to a curtailment of effect periods.

um" refers to reflections of feeling, extensive clarifications, and "clarifications plus"—i.e., those clarifications that have an additional element contributed by the therapist. "Far on the interpretive continuum" includes interventions that are didactic, information inquiries, reassurances, simple clarifications, etc.

Comparisons on nine variables yielded only one significant difference. As shown in Figure 1, close noninterpretations were, on the average, almost three times as long (63 words) as far noninterpretations ($p < .001$). Also included in Figure 1 are the mean numbers of patient words (516 and 545) and therapist words (109 and 89) following the two kinds of noninterpretations. These do not involve statistically significant findings, but are presented for illustrative purposes.

Figure 1 shows that each type of intervention is markedly shorter as one goes from comprehensive to moderate-limited interpretations to close to far noninterpretations. In the effect periods following these four types of input by therapists, patients talk increasingly more, but by far the greatest rise is associated with the step from the comprehensive to the moderate-limited category. In a partially complementary fashion, the activity of therapists in effect periods drops markedly as one proceeds from the comprehensive to the moderate-limited classification, but remains at a quite even level thereafter.

It is apparent that comprehensive interpretations are in a class by themselves, as compared to the other interventions. In view of this evidence, one is tempted to attribute our relevant major study findings to the uniqueness of comprehensive interpretations. But it is important to note that had our major study been confined to moderate-limited interpretations as compared with all noninterpretations, we would still have found that patients talked less after interpretations (on each of the three pertinent variables). The differences would, of course, have been much less distinctive (and probably not statistically significant).

In relation to form, then, comprehensive interpretations are themselves distinctive, and have some distinctive therapist and patient sequelae. Do they also distinctively influence the content of patient verbalization? Significant differences between responses of patients following comprehensive and moderate-limited interpretations were found on four out of 10 content variables. Means for them, based on the combined ratings of two judges, t-test values, and probabilities[3] are presented in Table 6.

TABLE 6

SIGNIFICANT DIFFERENCES IN CONTENT OF PATIENT MATERIAL FOLLOWING
COMPREHENSIVE AND MODERATE-LIMITED INTERPRETATIONS

Variable	Mean Following Comprehensive Interpretations (N = 12)	Mean Following Moderate-Limited Interpretations (N = 48)	t[a]	p[b]
Communication of conscious-level material	1.29	1.68	-2.68	<.005
Anger, hostility, or aggression	0.66	1.25	-2.27	<.025
Transference-related material	0.50	1.15	-2.06	<.025
Surprise	0.13	0.42	-1.76	< .05

[a]Minus signs indicate moderate-limited interpretations followed by greater amount of specified variable.

[b]Probabilities based on t (one-tailed test).

All of the tabled differences show less of the quality in question in effect periods following comprehensive interpretations as compared to effect periods following moderate-limited ones. The results for *Communication of conscious-level material* and *Transference-related material* may well be related to the form finding that patients talk less after comprehensive interpretations. Indeed, this same fact also may explain, although less directly, the other findings in Table 6. That is, because of reduced patient verbalization the opportunity for the manifestation of cognitive and affective

[3]One-tailed t tests were used to make possible comparisons with results from the main interpretation versus noninterpretation study, and on the assumption that comprehensive interpretations would be followed by more of the variable in question. However, even if two-tailed significance tests had been used, differences on the same four variables would have been found significant or nearly so (p <.01, <.05, <.05, <.10 respectively for variables listed in Table 6).

reactions may also have been reduced. However, this did not happen in our main study where interpretations, as contrasted with noninterpretations, were followed by fewer patient words. Despite this, interpretations were still followed by greater amounts of the various content variables in all instances where differences were significant. On the other hand, this point may not be apt, since three of the variables considered here—*Anger, Surprise*, and *Communication of conscious-level material*—did not involve significant differences in the main study. They were all somewhat greater, however, after noninterpretations. Here we see they were significantly greater after moderate-limited interpretations than after comprehensive ones. Thus, in both instances, these variables were more pronounced under the condition where the patient talked more. In view of these parallels, lack of opportunity may be at least a partial explanation for the present results.

One of the major hypotheses of this study was that patients communicate less relatively factual, conscious-level material after interpretations than after noninterpretations. If comprehensive interpretations represent the acme of interpretation, then presumably they are followed by less conscious-level material than are moderate-limited ones. Accordingly, the data showing that this is so for the present study are consistent with expectations. However, we would also anticipate that such outstanding interpretations would be followed by an increase in deeper-level associations of patients. But, according to our data, comprehensive and moderate-limited interpretations are not markedly different in regard to eliciting deeper-level material.

If similar reasoning is applied to the other findings shown in Table 6, then the data are not consistent with expectations, and comprehensive interpretations are not more effective than moderate-limited ones in eliciting *Transference-related material, Anger, hostility, or aggression*, and *Surprise*. The finding for *Transference-related material* is particularly nonconducive to emphasizing the pre-eminent merit of comprehensive interpretations. Their value would have been considerably enhanced, in psychoanalytic eyes, if they had been followed by more of such material, since dealing with the transference is assumed to be exceedingly important. The importance of the arousal of anger is more equivocal. Manifestation of hostility may be ameliorative or not, depending on a variety of factors, but this is not the postulate at issue here. The stimulus value of comprehensive interpretations is at issue, and they clearly are less anger-arousing than other types of interpretations. In view of the tiny amount of *Surprise* following comprehensive interpretations, the finding with regard to it is of more theoretical than therapeutic or practical interest. It seems likely that comprehensive interpretations are less surprising than moderate-limited ones because they often include many recapitulative and summary elements: much that the therapist specifically states in them may have been implied and adumbrated in earlier comments.

In fact, these characteristics of comprehensive interpretations may better account for all four of our positive findings than does lack of opportunity. Despite their rarity, comprehensive interpretations are frequently less novel and more final than moderate-limited ones, and may therefore be less stimulating, less arousing. In order not to lose sight of our several nonsignificant content findings, however, our general conclusion must be that comprehensive interpretations are less effective than moderate-limited interpretations in certain respects, and not appreciably different from them in others.

Our data so far have not suggested that comprehensive interpretations play a critical role in the psychotherapy process. However, we have not yet considered them from this point of view in connection with the major content findings of this research. Earlier, we found more affect, more understanding and insight, more defensive and oppositional associations, and more transference-related material after interpretations than after noninterpretations. Comprehensive and moderate-limited interpretations differed appreciably only in regard to the last of these—comprehensive interpretations were less effective than other interpretations in eliciting material related to the transference.

Altogether, the evidence does not support the special utility of comprehensive interpretations over other types of interpretations. Despite, or because of, their being the rarest, longest, and most complex interventions of the therapist, they do not appear to have uniquely valuable effects.

7

IMPLICATIONS OF THE STUDY

The data presented in the preceding chapters have indicated several ways in which interpretations are more effective than noninterpretations. Accordingly, this research has certain implications for clinical practice. These range from the relatively simple to the more involved. If for some reason a therapist wishes his patient to respond to him less quickly and talk less, he is more likely to achieve these goals by making an interpretation than by using some other type of intervention. Similarly, if a therapist is interested in having his patient manifest affect or understanding or defensiveness, or talk about the transference, he is likely to elicit more of any of these reactions if he interprets, rather than if he clarifies, instructs, asks for information, etc. The suggestion about affect requires a cautionary note, however, inasmuch as we were unable to tap (and document) the specific type of affect that is likely to increase after interpretations.

Some other cautions are also in order in connection with these generalizations. A particular effect cannot be guaranteed to occur, or to be greater, in any one particular instance. Thus, if a therapist makes an interpretation with the purpose of having his patient associate more to the transference, for example, he may or may not elicit this response on a given occasion. Nevertheless, it is more probable that the therapist will achieve his goal by the use of an interpretation than by some other intervention. In this context, we may emphasize that this study has explored interpretations as a type of intervention, and we have not further coded them according to their specific subject matter. Further information about the relationship between the latter and particular patient reactions would, of course, be of considerable interest.

Another caution, closely related to the preceding one, merits attention. Note that the several response qualities that are generally increased after interpretations may or may not occur together in specific instances. Pending further analysis of our correlational data, we can only say that affect, understanding, defensiveness, and transference-related material are not highly related. And after a *particular* interpretation, none, any, or all of these responses may or may not be increased.

It is also necessary to recognize that the several reaction qualities mentioned above are not exclusive to interpretations. That is, our generalizations should not be taken to imply that only interpretations are followed by silence, affect, defensiveness, etc. The data do indicate that comparatively greater amounts of certain qualities are shown immediately after interpretations than after noninterpretations, but this does not mean that the latter elicit zero amounts of the phenomena in question.

Our findings may suggest certain sequences to the clinician for his interpretations and noninterpretations. To illustrate: suppose a patient is on the verge of uncovering some important repressed material. We know that interpretations typically reduce patient verbalization. Therefore, by making a noninterpretation rather than an interpretation at this point, the therapist is more likely to encourage verbalization, and, hopefully, verbalization of the repressed. If his patient is to understand this new material, the therapist now may do well to make an interpretation, rather than a noninterpretation. On the other hand, he probably should make a noninterpretation if he is more concerned with not arousing his patient's defensiveness. A better situation for the therapist probably would be one in which he could elicit increased understanding without increased defensiveness. Although these reactions do not tend to occur together, our data indicate that both of them are likely to be greater after interpretations than after noninterpretations. In view of this, the therapist must decide which reaction he prizes most at a given moment in the therapeutic transaction, and interpret, or not, accordingly.

Despite our frequent reference to the greater effectiveness of interpretations, so far we have not discussed their therapeutic value. To establish definitively the merit of interpretation in therapy presupposes a theory of the curative process. If the arousal of certain reactions in patients is known to be therapeutic, and if interpretations stimulate such reactions more markedly than do other interventions, then interpretations are of demonstrable value. In terms of the several differential results presented in this study, if more silence, more understanding, etc., are viewed as favorable phenomena, then interpretation, as an effective eliciting agent for such phenomena, is a pre-eminently useful ameliorative tool. If not only the arousal but the *extent* of the arousal of certain reactions determines therapeutic effectiveness, then the evaluative problem is more complex. While expression of affect, for example, may be a general desideratum, there is perhaps an optimal amount of such expression that is most contributory to therapeutic gain. In such an instance, it is possible that "less" affect is more beneficial than "more" affect. The lack of known cutoff points rules out precise, but not general, consideration of this important concept. In connection with absolute quantities, recall that all the affective and cognitive qualities studied, regardless of whether they followed interpretations or noninterpretations, tended not to be strongly manifested.

In view of our psychoanalytic orientation, it is appropriate to appraise interpretations primarily in this theoretical framework. Three of the positive results reported here refer to auspicious processes in psychoanalytic formulations. While it is undesirable to have patients flooded or overwhelmed by too much affect, the expression of affect is advocated by analysts. Our finding that interpretations elicited relatively more affect—but also, clearly, not an extreme amount—attests to one advantage of interpretation as a therapeutic technique. More, rather than less, understanding and insight was also associated with interpretations, and is favored by analytic theory. It is probable that no upper limit exists for the amount of this response that is desirable. On the assumption that it is through analysis of the transference that therapeutic progress is achieved, interpretations again have the theoretically preferred effect in that they stimulated greater reference to such material.

Which type of intervention is favored by the finding that more defensive and oppositional associations followed interpretations than noninterpretations? Nonanalytic theorists perceive manifestations of resistance as detrimental to therapeutic progress. Analysts assume that some form of resistance will inevitably occur in any therapy, and they interpret this resistance to decrease it and to increase the patient's self-knowledge. Accordingly, defensiveness on the part of the patient need not be disruptive. Despite this tolerance, analysts also probably prefer less, rather than more, defensive and oppositional associations. From this point of view, interpretations are less beneficial than noninterpretations.

Other positive findings of this research pertain to the form of reactions by patients: patients talked less after interpretations, and responded more slowly to interpretations than to noninterpretations. To the extent that these reactions are viewed as manifestations of resistance, and therefore as hindrances to therapy, so may interpretation be judged as a disruptive intervention technique. On the other hand, decreased patient verbalization and slower response time may be therapeutically desirable, as demonstrating trust and comfort in the therapist-patient interaction, or impingement on a psychologically meaningful area, or concentration on thinking something through. However, these several inferences are more speculative and more equivocal than those concerning the content of patient responses, and therefore it is difficult to weigh them in the present context. Our general conclusion is that interpretations have several effects that are therapeutically desirable, at least one that may be undesirable, and others that may either facilitate or impede therapeutic progress. This tally suggests that the therapeutic assets of interpretation outweigh its limitations.

APPENDIX A

TABLE 7

DESCRIPTION OF CASES[a]

Identification of Case	Number of Hours of Therapy	
Case 1[b]	164	Psychoanalytically oriented psychotherapy, two meetings a week Therapist: Female—senior training and supervising psychoanalyst Patient: Female in early 30s
Case 2	315	Psychoanalysis, four meetings a week Therapist: Male—psychoanalyst Patient: Female in early 20s
Case 3	655	Psychoanalysis, five meetings a week Therapist: Male—psychoanalyst Patient: Female in early 30s
Case 4	34	Psychoanalytically oriented psychotherapy, one meeting a week Therapist: Male—training psychoanalyst Patient: Male in early 20s

[a]Material from these cases is also treated in Sklansky et al. (1966).

[b]This case was still in process at the time of the study. It was terminated after 237 hours.

APPENDIX B

VERBATIM EXAMPLES FROM PSYCHO-THERAPY HOURS OF COMPREHENSIVE, MODERATE, AND LIMITED INTER-PRETATIONS; AND CLOSE AND FAR NONINTERPRETATIONS[1]

A Comprehensive Interpretation

What, ah, oh, on the contrary. Ah, you've ah, ah, lately we've seen how your anxiety, ah, the anxiety you have here with me, ah, around the matter of wishing to be thought of as an attractive woman instead of a little girl, about having sexual feelings regarding me, and I think there's, we're going to see that this anxiety is because you're reliving something. You've indicated the struggle you had in your adolescence, your early adolescence, a struggle having to do, one, with your, that you, that you felt that your mother didn't want you to show such interests. Also, you talked about how when you saw yourself as a young woman, as a developing adolescent female, had a wish to be attractive, and ah, as all girls experience you turned your interest toward men. The man in your home was your stepfather, who belonged to your mother, which put you in a situation of rivalry with your mother. And made you feel guilty. Even if he was just nice to you, because that stirred up your fantasies, of what more you might have wanted, if, ah, from him because of the growing feelings you were having at that time. Now, a-ah, at first as you have indicated you reacted to all this by acting as if you weren't interested in it, and then making yourself obscure, ah, in this way. And then because you felt,

---

[1] Transcribed from tape recordings of therapy sessions.

73

ah, ah, your feelings of guilt connected with sexual issues, such as to be attractive and desirable, you allowed yourself that occasionally when you could suffer, to take care of the feeling of guilt. A guilt stemming from the earlier fantasies of your adolescence, fantasies related to your attraction to your stepfather. And the rivalry that put you in with your mother. And here, every time ah, here with me, every time you're on the verge of expressing something of such wishes, you get anxious. And you take flight into your being a little girl, or being inconsequential, or being ignored, to obscure these wishes and the fantasies associated with them, because you're, you re-experience, revive the memory of your jealous conflict, where it was laden with ah, the feelings of guilt about the fantasies you had for your stepfather and the competition with your ah, mother. The competition it would put you in with your mother. This is the sort of thing that every young woman goes through ah, she begins to feel ah, the development and growth of herself as a woman and ah, wanting to be desirable and having these feelings. And the stirring up of fantasies. Now, I think you get so caught up in the feelings associated with this that you kind of go, ah, ah, stop talking here. I think you, you lose sight of the fact that ah, ah, you don't differentiate me as I am today, and you as you are today, from the memory you're reliving. The memory of the earlier experience of such feelings in relation to your stepfather, and in connection with your mother.

A Moderate Interpretation

Well, I don't think it's so vague. I think you're trying very hard to uh, uh, separate personality into male and female almost as if you're a little bit afraid to find any female in yourself. See, as soon as you see any weakness, you—for instance, you don't like the kind of weakness that these girls have—that they don't stand up for themselves. You object to weakness. You objected to that in yourself too. Also, now you're objecting to the fact that these girls don't stay on their side of the, their side of the fence. See? They should recognize they, they are females. Which means then that you, you don't want to feel that there's any intrusion into your male concept of yourself. You don't want to let anybody mix things up. Now I think that what's important here—very important for you to know that—is that there is some anxiety within you, if you discover anything which smacks of the weak or the female (patient statement) within yourself.

A Limited Interpretation

Understandable that you have this (clears throat) emotional response to—a change, but the intensity of your response ah, ah, is one ah—is of such a nature that you, you seem to be responding as if in fact you were, you were a helpless little girl. The intensity of the responses based on the ah, an anachronism of your, your view of yourself.

A "Close" Noninterpretation (close to interpretations on the interpretive continuum)

Well, in both situations you've kind of taken a position of the underprivileged one. In this last one it is the wives—um?

A "Far" Noninterpretation (far from interpretations on the interpretive continuum)

Except that she doesn't know whether her birth, eh, uh, uh—a morning party or a Friday party would have been—it's—the only thing she knows is a party, isn't that right? (Patient statement.) Th-this is what I wanted you to talk about.

APPENDIX C

TWO RATED EXCERPTS OF PATIENT MATERIAL[1]

Excerpt 1

P 31: Because, well, the whole thing is that I, I just think that if a woman expresses, you know, I mean, not that a woman should go around expressing to just anybody how she feels about sleeping with her husband, or something like that. I, you know, but I mean, I think, I just, not that I think this is re—, is rational but, ah, but I just feel that a woman (clears throat) expresses her own sexual desires and expresses ah, just a desire, a healthy desire for sex. I mean, she doesn't (clears throat), doesn't have to talk, you know, say the words but, but, you know, whatever way there is of communicating to a man that, that, you, you're receptive and you'll enjoy it and things like that. But I just get the feeling that rather than this being a healthy woman, that she is sort of, ah, what's that word they call women who are, you know, who have too much sex, nymphomaniacs, I guess. That if, you know, if she expresses any desire that, that it's abnormal, you know.

P 32: Well, what I'm saying, I, I don't, you know, that, that, I know differently, you know, intellectually and I know this isn't true but. . .

---

[1] These excerpts from psychotherapy hours have been slightly changed for publication to assure anonymity.
Ratings are based on average of two independent ratings.

76

P 33 (15-second pause): Well, but that still doesn't, I mean, that still doesn't, well, I mean, I haven't come here with that problem (laughs). And now, you mean, now I have another problem to solve because well, well, that isn't what I mean, but well, it's hard to explain. But see, like I was thinking last night (clears throat) and I was trying to figure out, you know, about it. And I was thinking, well, that isn't my problem. My problem isn't that, that, you know, my problem isn't that I'm in love with you and that you can't love me back because you're my analyst and, and so, now do I have that problem? Now, do I have to work out that problem? You know, I, I can't explain it but I, but I just don't get it. I mean, okay, so if that's true, then, then, then where does it fit into the whole thing? I mean, no, I don't suppose you do, because I don't know what I mean either, but (sighs)—which means that the answer to my question is that I saw you as a romantic figure?

P 34: Well, is that because I mean, just because you're a man and, and I have certain feelings of, I mean, well, I mean, these feelings are feelings that, that, sometimes, I wish you would give me more attention in the form of, being here all the time and, and things like that. Well, well, is that really how, you know, how I'm identifying you with "X"? That, you know, that maybe some-times, I have the same feelings about him as you? (21-second pause.)

Ratings for Excerpt 1

Presence of affect	2.5	Communication of deeper-	
Anxiety	2.0	level material	2.0
Anger, hostility, or		Blocking	1.5
aggression	0	Defensive and opposition-	
Depression	0	al associations	1.0
Pleasant affect	0.5	Understanding and insight	1.5
Surprise	0.5	Transference-related	
Ego dysfunctioning	1.0	material	3.0
Symptomatology	0.5		
Communication of con-			
scious-level material	1.0		

Excerpt 2

P 27: Oh, God! Th-this was definitely a truth (sigh).

P 28: Mmm-hmm.

P 29: Yeah.

P 30: Mmm. Well, what you're saying is then that this is some-thing that, uh, I need more help with.

P 31: Well, what you're probably preparing me for is a recur-rence of this only on a more important scale. I mean, something that, uh, happens again only, only it'll be more important to me. Perhaps, I will have fallen in love with the girl, something like that. Well, this I suppose is true.

P 32: Well (clears throat) I have heard that such a thing as this you don't really get out of your system. That this is, uh, pretty, uh, well ingrained and that, uh—by golly, eh, for the rest of my life quite probably, as a general rule, I won't be attracted to any other kind of woman but the woman that falls into that category—that fits that description.

P 33: Mmm-hmm. (22-second pause.) Yes, I'm aware of this (sigh), this distance I've put between myself and others.

P 34: I, I probably did. However, there were some days—well, practically most of the time, I was pretty anxious to talk to you.

P 35: Pretty anxious to talk things over. 'Cause today I certainly was after this recent incident, I was anxious to talk to you. But, uh, perhaps, I did—I don't know. Well, yes, it's, it's—I've always been aware of the difficulty I've had with being—feeling friendly toward—really friendly—really fond of people. I'm very fond of this fellow named "X." We've become very good friends—but, as I pointed out, we've known each other for six years. And it's taken four years for us to really become good friends. I think he's a lot the way I—like the way I am, I would suspect—perhaps, not.

Ratings for Exercpt 2

Presence of affect	2.5	Communication of deeper-level material	2.5
Anxiety	2.0		
Anger, hostility, or aggression	0.5	Blocking	1.0
Depression	1.0	Defensive and oppositional associations	0.5
Pleasant affect	1.5	Understanding and insight	2.0
Surprise	0.5	Transference-related material	0.5
Ego dysfunctioning	1.0		
Symptomatology	0		
Communication of conscious-level material	1.0		

BIBLIOGRAPHY

Adams, H. E., Butler, J. R., & Noblin, C. D. (1962), Effects of Psychoanalytically-Derived Interpretations: A Verbal Conditioning Paradigm? *Psychol. Rep.*, 10:691-694.

Alexander, F., & French, T. M. (1946), *Psychoanalytic Therapy: Principles and Application.* New York: Ronald Press.

Auld, F., & White, A. M. (1959), Sequential Dependencies in Psychotherapy. *J. Abnorm. Soc. Psychol.*, 58:100-104.

Bales, R. F. (1950), *Interaction Process Analysis: A Method for the Study of Small Groups.* Cambridge, Mass.: Addison-Wesley Press.

Bell, J. E. (1948), *Projective Techniques.* New York: Longmans, Green.

Bergman, D. V. (1951), Counseling Method and Client Responses. *J. Consult. Psychol.*, 15:216-224.

Bibring, E. (1954), Psychoanalysis and the Dynamic Therapies. *J. Amer. Psychoanal. Assn.*, 2:745-770.

Brenner, C. (1955), *An Elementary Textbook of Psychoanalysis.* New York: International Universities Press.

Butler, J. R. (1962), Behavioral Analysis of Psychoanalytically Derived Interpretations Presented on Operant Schedules of Reinforcement. *Dissertation Abstr.*, 23(3):1069-1070.

Cartwright, R. D. (1966), A Comparison of the Response to Psychoanalytic and Client-Centered Psychotherapy. In *Methods of Research in Psychotherapy*, ed. L. A. Gottschalk & A. H. Auerbach. New York: Appleton-Century-Crofts, pp. 517-529.

Christiansen, B. (1964), The Scientific Status of Psychoanalytic Clinical Evidence. *Inquiry*, 7:47-79.

Cohen, R. A., & Cohen, M. B. (1961), Research in Psychotherapy: A Preliminary Report. *Psychiatry*, 24, Suppl. 2:46-61.

Colby, K. M. (1951), *A Primer for Psychotherapists.* New York: Ronald Press.

_____ (1961), On the Greater Amplifying Power of Causal-Correlative over Interrogative Inputs on Free-Association in an Experimental Psychoanalytic Situation. *J. Nerv. Ment. Dis.*, 133:233-239.

Dibner, A. S. (1958), Ambiguity and Anxiety. *J. Abnorm. Soc. Psychol.*, 56:165-174.

Dittman, A. T. (1952), The Interpersonal Process in Psychotherapy: Development of a Research Method. *J. Abnorm. Soc. Psychol.*, 47:236-244.

Frank, G. H., & Sweetland, A. (1962), A Study of the Process of Psychotherapy: The Verbal Interaction. *J. Consult. Psychol.*, 26:135-138.

Freud, S. (1937), Constructions in Analysis. *Standard Edition*, 23:257-269. London: Hogarth Press, 1964.

Fromm-Reichmann, F. (1951), *Principles of Intensive Psychotherapy.* Chicago: University of Chicago Press.

Gillespie, J. F., Jr. (1953), Verbal Signs of Resistance in Client-Centered Therapy. In *Group Report of a Program of Research in Psychotherapy*, ed. W. U. Snyder. State College, Pa.: Pennsylvania State University, pp. 105-119.

80

Greenson, R. R. (1959), The Classic Psychoanalytic Approach. In *American Handbook of Psychiatry*, Vol. 2, ed. S. Arieti. New York: Basic Books, pp. 1399-1416.

Grossman, D. (1952), An Experimental Investigation of a Psychotherapeutic Technique. *J. Consult. Psychol.*, 16:325-331.

Haggard, E. A. (1958), *Intraclass Correlation and the Analysis of Variance*. New York: Dryden Press.

———— Hiken, J. R., & Isaacs, K. S. (1965), Some Effects of Recording and Filming on the Psychotherapeutic Process. *Psychiatry*, 28:169-191.

Hobbs, N. (1962), Sources of Gain in Psychotherapy. *Amer. Psychol.*, 17:741-747.

Isaacs, S. (1939), Criteria for Interpretations. *Int. J. Psycho-Anal.*, 20:148-160.

Jones, E. (1946), A Valedictory Address. *Int. J. Psycho-Anal.*, 27:7-12.

Kanfer, F. H., Phillips, J. S., Matarazzo, J. D., & Saslow, G. (1960), Experimental Modification of Interviewer Content in Standardized Interviews. *J. Consult. Psychol.*, 24:528-536.

Kubie, L. S. (1960), *Practical and Theoretical Aspects of Psychoanalysis*. New York: Praeger.

Lennard, H. L., & Bernstein, A. (1960), *The Anatomy of Psychotherapy*. New York: Columbia University Press.

Levitov, E. S. (1965), Immediate Effects on Patients of Psychoanalytic Interpretations. Unpublished doctoral dissertation, University of Chicago.

Levy, L. H. (1963), *Psychological Interpretation*. New York: Holt, Rinehart & Winston.

Loewenstein, R. M. (1963), Some Considerations on Free Association. *J. Amer. Psychoanal. Assn.*, 2:451-473.

Mahl, G. F. (1961), Measures of Two Expressive Aspects of a Patient's Speech in Two Psychotherapeutic Interviews. In *Comparative Psycholinguistic Analysis of Two Psychotherapeutic Interviews*, ed. L. A. Gottschalk. New York: International Universities Press, pp. 91-114.

Menninger, K. (1958), *Theory of Psychoanalytic Technique*. New York: Basic Books.

Miller, A. A., Isaacs, K. S., & Haggard, E. A. (1965), On the Nature of the Observing Function of the Ego. *Brit. J. Med. Psychol.*, 38:161-169.

Murphy, W. F. (1958), A Comparison of Psychoanalysis with the Dynamic Psychotherapies. *J. Nerv. Ment. Dis.*, 126:441-450.

Palombo, S. R., & Bruch, H. (1964), Falling Apart: The Verbalization of Ego Failure. *Psychiatry*, 27:248-258.

Paul, L. (1963), *Psychoanalytic Clinical Interpretation*. New York: Free Press of Glencoe.

Pope, B., & Siegman, A. W. (1962), The Effect of Therapist Verbal Activity Level and Specificity on Patient Productivity and Speech Disturbances in the Initial Interview. *J. Consult. Psychol.*, 26:489.

Rogers, C. R. (1942), *Counseling and Psychotherapy*. Boston: Houghton Mifflin.

———— & Rablen, R. (1958), *A Scale of Process in Psychotherapy*. Mimeographed manual, University of Wisconsin.

Saul, L. J. (1958), *Technique and Practice of Psychoanalysis*. Philadelphia: Lippincott.

Sherman, D. (1945), An Analysis of the Dynamic Relationship between Counselor Techniques and Outcomes in Longer Units of the Interview Situation. Unpublished doctoral dissertation, Ohio State University.

Shulman, J. L., Kaspar, J. C., & Barger, P. M. (1964), *The Therapeutic Dialogue*. Springfield, Ill. : Charles C Thomas.

Sklansky, M. A., Isaacs, K. S., & Haggard, E. A. (1960), A Method for the Study of Verbal Interaction and Levels of Meaning in Psychotherapy. *Scientific Papers and Discussions*, American Psychiatric Association, District Branches Publication 1, pp. 133-148.

———— ———— Levitov, E. S., & Haggard, E. A. (1966), Verbal Interaction and Levels of Meaning in Psychotherapy. *Arch. Gen. Psychiat.*, 14:158-170.

Slater, R., ed. (1956), Karen Horney on Psychoanalytic Technique: Interpretations. *Amer. J. Psychoanal.*, 16:118-124.

Snyder, W. U. (1945), An Investigation of the Nature of Nondirective Psychotherapy. *J. Gen. Psychol.*, 33:193-223.

_____ (1963), *Dependency in Psychotherapy.* New York: Macmillan.

Speisman, J. C. (1957), The Relationship between Depth of Interpretation and Verbal Expressions of Resistance in Psychotherapy. Unpublished doctoral dissertation, University of Michigan.

Strachey, J. (1934), The Nature of the Therapeutic Action of Psycho-Analysis. In *Psychoanalytic Clinical Interpretation,* ed. L. Paul. New York: Free Press of Glencoe, 1963.

Sullivan, H. S. (1947), *Conceptions of Modern Psychiatry.* Washington, D.C.: William Alanson White Psychiatric Foundation.

Tarachow, S. (1963), *An Introduction to Psychotherapy.* New York: International Universities Press.

INDEX

Adams, H. E., 10
Affect
  morbid or dysphoric; see Depression
  pleasant, 12, 44, 49, 51, 53, 56, 58, 59
  presence of, 10-11, 44, 49, 50, 52, 56-60, 67-70
Aggression; see Anger
Alexander, F., 11
Anger, hostility, and aggression, 11, 44, 48, 51, 53, 54, 56, 58, 65-67
Anxiety, 11, 44, 48, 53, 56, 58, 60
Associations
  blocking of; see Blocking
  defensive and oppositional; see Defensive and oppositional associations
Auld, F., 9, 10, 14, 39, 54

Bales, R. F., 19
Barger, P. M., 14
Bell, J. E., 9
Bergman, D. V., 14
Bernstein, A., 9-11, 39, 57
Bibring, E., 11, 12, 14, 16
Blocking, 14, 45, 48, 53, 58, 60
Brenner, C., 12
Bruch, H., 12
Butler, J. R., 10

Cartwright, R. D., 14, 19
Christiansen, B., 13
Cohen, M. B., 14
Cohen, R. A., 14
Colby, K. M., 10, 12, 28
Conscious-level material, communication of, 13, 44, 49, 50, 53, 57, 58, 65, 66

Deeper-level material, communication of, 13, 44, 49, 50, 53, 55, 57, 66
Defensive and oppositional associations, 14, 45, 49-54, 58-60, 67-71
Depression and morbid or dysphoric affect, 11, 44, 51, 53, 56
Dibner, A. S., 11
Dittman, A. T., 14

Effect periods, 7-8, 26-27
  curtailed, 27, 40, 63
  therapist activity in, 28-33
  see also Interpretations, patient verbalization in response to
Ego disfunctioning, 12, 44, 48, 53, 58, 60
Explanation; see Interpretations
Frank, G. H., 13, 14
French, T. M., 11
Freud, S., 13
Fromm-Reichmann, F., 11

Gillespie, J. F., Jr., 14
Greenson, R. R., 11, 12
Grossman, D., 14

Haggard, E. A., 5, 47
Hobbs, N., 55
Horney, K., 11
Hostility; see Anger

Insight; see Understanding and insight
Interpretations
  comprehensive, 17-18, 25, 26, 55, 61-67
  content of patients' responses to, 49-60, 64-65
  definition of, 16-18
  differing opinions about, 3
  effectiveness of, and clinical practice, 68-71
  experimental study of, design and procedures, 4-8, 19-29, 35-37, 43-48; methodological limitations of, 59-60
  hypotheses concerning, 8-15
  immediate effects of, 7
  individual differences in patients' responses to, 40-41, 58-59
  in effect periods, 29, 31-32, 62-63
  length of, 28-30, 32-34, 41, 62-64
  moderate-limited, 17, 18, 25, 26, 55, 61-67
  noninterpretations versus, 5-14, 69-71

83

ABOUT THE AUTHORS

EDITH LEVITOV GARDUK received her Ph.D. in clinical psychology from the University of Chicago in 1965. At that time she was Research Associate on the Psychotherapy Project of the Neuropsychiatric Institute, University of Illinois. Her research and clinical training includes two summers at the National Institute of Mental Health while she was a graduate student, and an internship at Billings Hospital of the University of Chicago. Since 1967 she has been Associate Director of the Howard University Counseling Service.

ERNEST A. HAGGARD received his Ph.D. from Harvard in 1946. He has held faculty positions at Harvard, the University of California (Berkeley), the University of Chicago, and the University of Illinois at the Medical Center, where he is currently professor of psychology in the Department of Psychiatry and holds a Career Research Award from the National Institute of Mental Health. His major interest is in learning and personality theory; he has also published in such areas as statistics and research methodology, the psychotherapy process, and the effects of social isolation.